Practice *Planners*™

Arthur E. Jongsma,

Helping therapists help their clients...

Practice *Planners*

Second Edition

THE COMPLETE ADULT
PSYCHOTHERAPY
Treatment Planner

A new, fully revised edition of the bestselling *The Complete Psychotherapy Treatment Planner*, this invaluable resource features:

• Treatment plan components for 39 behaviorally based problems—including five completely new problem sets

• A step-by-step guide to writing treatment plans

• Over 500 additional prewritten treatment goals, objectives, and interventions

• Handy workbook format with space to record your own treatment plan options

• Over 100,000 Practice *Planners* sold

Arthur E. Jongsma, Jr., and L. Mark Peterson

Practice *Planners*
Arthur E. Jongsma, Jr., Series Editor

Brief Therapy
HOMEWORK
PLANNER

• Contains 62 ready-to-copy homework assignments that can be used to facilitate brief individual therapy

• Homework assignments and exercises are keyed to over 30 behaviorally-based presenting problems from *The Complete Psychotherapy Treatment Planner*

• Assignments may be quickly customized using the enclosed disk

• Over 100,000 Practice *Planners* sold

Gary M. Schultheis

Practice *Planners*

The Clinical
DOCUMENTATION
SOURCEBOOK
Second Edition

A Comprehensive Collection of
Mental Health Practice
Forms, Handouts, and Records

—— **FEATURES** ——

• Contains ready-to-use form for managing the mental health treatment process

• Covers every stage of the treatment process

• Includes customizable forms on disk

• Over 100,000 Practice *Planners* sold

Donald E. Wiger

Practice *Planners*
Arthur E. Jongsma, Jr., Series Editor

The Adult Psychotherapy
PROGRESS NOTES PLANNER

This time-saving resource:

Contains Progress notes customize to for 39 behaviorally-based problems

Covers the gamut of possible outcomes for every intervention suggested in the best-selling Complete Adult Psychotherapy Treatment Planner, 2nd Edition

Includes 1,000s of prewritten sratient and patient presentation descriptions

Provides a handy workbook format with space to record your own progress note options

Over 180,000 Practice *Planners* sold

Arthur E. Jongsma, Jr.

Practice*Planners*™ Order Form

Treatment Planners cover all the necessary elements for developing formal treatment plans, including detailed problem definitions, long-term goals, short-term objectives, therapeutic interventions, and DSM-IV diagnoses.

Documentation Sourcebooks provide all the forms and records you need to meet the documentation requirements of the managed care era. All of the documents are also provided on disk so they can be easily customized.

The Complete Adult Psychotherapy Treatment Planner, Second Edition
0-471-31924-4 / $39.95

The Child Psychotherapy Treatment Planner, Second Edition
0-471-34764-7 / $39.95

The Adolescent Psychotherapy Treatment Planner, Second Edition
0-471-34766-3 / $39.95

The Chemical Dependence Treatment Planner
0-471-23795-7 / $39.95

The Continuum of Care Treatment Planner
0-471-19568-5 / $39.95

The Couples Psychotherapy Treatment Planner
0-471-24711-1 / $39.95

The Employee Assistance (EAP) Treatment Planner
0-471-24709-X / $39.95

The Pastoral Counseling Treatment Planner
0-471-25416-9 / $39.95

The Older Adult Psychotherapy Treatment Planner
0-471-29574-4 / $39.95

The Behavioral Medicine Treatment Planner
0-471-31923-6 / $39.95

The Gay and Lesbian Psychotherapy Treatment Planner
0-471-35080-X / $39.95

The Clinical Documentation Sourcebook, Second Edition
0-471-32692-5 / $49.95

The Psychotherapy Documentation Primer
0-471-28990-6 / $45.00

The Couple and Family Clinical Documentation Sourcebook
0-471-25234-4 / $49.95

The Clinical Child Documentation Sourcebook
0-471-29111-0 / $49.95

The Chemical Dependence Treatment Documentation Sourcebook
0-471-31285-1 / $49.95

The Forensic Documentation Sourcebook
0-471-25459-2 / $85.00

The Continuum of Care Clinical Documentation Sourcebook
0-471-34581-4 / $75.00

NEW AND FORTHCOMING

The Group Therapy Treatment Planner
0-471-37449-0 / $39.95

The Family Therapy Treatment Planner
0-471-34768-X / $39.95

The Severe and Persistent Mental Illness Treatment Planner
0-471-35945-9 / $39.95

The Mental Retardation and Developmental Disability Treatment Planner
0-471-38253-1 / $39.95

The Social Work and Human Services Treatment Planner
0-471-37741-4 / $39.95 (12/00)

The Neuropsychological Treatment Planner
0-471-35178-4 / $39.95 (3/01)

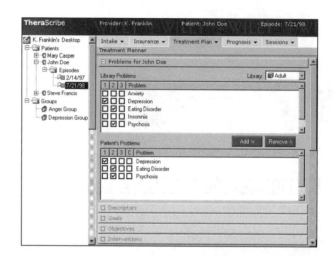

Chemical Dependence Treatment Homework Planner

Chemical Dependence Treatment Homework Planner

James R. Finley
Brenda S. Lenz

John Wiley & Sons, Inc.

New York • Chichester • Weinheim • Brisbane • Singapore • Toronto

Note about Photocopy Rights

The publisher grants purchasers permission to reproduce handouts from this book for professional use with their clients.

Library of Congress Cataloging-in-Publication Data:

Finley, James R., 1958–
    Chemical dependence treatment homework planner / James R. Finley and Brenda S. Lenz.
        p.   cm. — (Practice planners)
    Includes bibliographical references.
    ISBN 0-471-32452-3 (paper/disk : alk. paper)
    1. Substance abuse—Treatment—Planning.   2. Substance abuse—Prevention—Problems, exercises, etc.   I. Lenz, Brenda S.   II. Title.   III. Series.
    RC564.15.F557   1999
    616.86'06—dc21   99-17989
                                                                                          CIP

Printed in the United States of America.

10 9 8 7 6 5 4 3

Practice Planner Series Preface

The practice of psychotherapy has a dimension that did not exist 30, 20, or even 15 years ago—accountability. Treatment programs, public agencies, clinics, and even group and solo practitioners must now justify the treatment of patients to outside review entities that control the payment of fees. This development has resulted in an explosion of paperwork.

Clinicians must now document what has been done in treatment, what is planned for the future, and what the anticipated outcomes of the interventions are. The books and software in this Practice Planner series are designed to help practitioners fulfill these documentation requirements efficiently and professionally.

The Practice Planner series is growing rapidly. It now includes not only the *Complete Adult Psychotherapy Treatment Planner,* Second Edition, and the *Child and Adolescent Psychotherapy Treatment Planner,* but also *Treatment Planners* targeted to specialty areas of practice, including: chemical dependency, the continuum of care, couples therapy, older adult treatment, employee assistance, behavioral medicine, pastoral counseling, family therapy, group therapy, and more.

In addition to the *Treatment Planners,* the series also includes *TheraScribe®: The Computerized Assistant to Psychotherapy Treatment Planning* and *TheraBiller™: The Computerized Mental Health Office Manager,* as well as adjunctive books, such as the *Brief Therapy, Chemical Dependence, Couples, Child,* and *Adolescent Homework Planners, The Psychotherapy Documentation Primer,* and *Clinical, Forensic, Child, Couples and Family,* and *Chemical Dependence Documentation Sourcebooks*—containing forms and resources to aid in mental health practice management. The goal of the series is to provide practitioners with the resources they need in order to provide high-quality care in the era of accountability—or, to put it simply, we seek to help you spend more time on patients, and less on paperwork.

ARTHUR E. JONGSMA, JR.
Grand Rapids, Michigan

This book is dedicated to all the hardworking clinicians who make it their vocation to help the millions of individuals and families afflicted with alcoholism and addiction. The ripples of your work will still be lapping at distant shores when all of us are gone and forgotten.

Contents

CONTENTS

Disk Contents

Preface

THE ROLE OF THERAPEUTIC HOMEWORK

In today's climate of managed care and leaner benefits packages, chemical dependence treatment providers must find ways to achieve measurable success in less time with less client contact, and often with clients whose problems are more complex and acute than we saw even five years ago. This means that much of the work must be done not during but between therapy sessions. Actually, this is often more effective than the residential mode of treatment that was standard a decade ago, because the client is rehearsing his or her new lifestyle in the environment where it will be put to the test, rather than in a sheltered treatment program. When problems come up in the process of reentry to the community, the client is still in the midst of treatment, with all the support and coaching that makes change possible.

However, this means we need to have effective homework assignments to give clients to carry out that between-sessions work. We have been struck on numerous occasions by the amount of time we spend creating relevant and interesting therapeutic homework assignments for our clients, and by the way good pieces of work get passed around and used by more and more clinicians. On more than one occasion each of us has been grateful that someone else has created a handout we needed for use with a client. That, on a wider scale, is the goal of this book and software package. The assignments in this book include cognitive-behavioral, brief therapy, psychodynamic, and Twelve-Step-based tasks for clients who are either abusing drugs (including alcohol) or are addicted. Within this eclectic blend of proven approaches, we hope to provide something for any substance-abusing client you may encounter. These assignments aim to do the following:

- Help clients realize that the responsibility for their recovery ultimately rests in their own hands—that we can support their efforts but we can't get clean and sober for them. By giving a client tasks to accomplish away from the clinician, we aim to eliminate the mind-set that says solving the problem is the clinician's role.
- Constantly draw on the clients' normal lives and routines for the resources with which they will work. The more realistic the rehearsals, the better the chance of success later in treatment and after graduation from a treatment program.

- Personalize the treatment and make it unique to each client; the nature of these homework assignments is such that if ten clients take the same therapeutic homework handout home, when they bring it back no two will have approached it in exactly the same way. As we get to know each client, we can tailor our approach to his or her personality and situation.

USING THIS BOOK

You can use this book in several ways. First, to locate the exercise you want, you can either look at the titles in the table of contents, open the book to the section relating to your client's problem and objective, or use the quick and easy cross-reference table provided, looking up the issue on which you're working and getting a list of the exercises that relate to that issue. Finally, you can also use the electronic copies enclosed on disk to customize our files by rewording items or adding a logo or other art or decoration. For further instructions on the enclosed disk please see the "About the Disk" section on pages 301–302.

If you have any suggestions for improvement, or want to tell us about a feature you especially like, please contact us via this publisher. We'd appreciate all the feedback we can get.

Section I

Understanding the Problem and Addressing Denial

What Does Abuse/ Addiction Mean to Me?

GOALS OF THE EXERCISE

1. To increase the client's awareness of his or her patterns of substance use.
2. To define the nature of the problem of substance abuse or addiction.
3. To help the client understand how the process of abuse/addiction has worked in his or her life.

TYPES OF PROBLEMS THIS EXERCISE MAY BE MOST USEFUL FOR

- Adult Children of Alcoholic (ACOA) Traits
- Blaming/Projection/Failure to Take Appropriate Responsibility
- Denial/Rationalization/Minimization of Substance-Abusing Behavior and/or Relapse Risk
- Generalized Treatment Resistance
- History of Self-Medication for Mood/Pain Problems
- Issues of Identity
- Learned Helplessness
- Living Environment Deficiencies (Relapse Triggers, Lack of Emotional Support, etc.)
- Low Self-Esteem
- Peer Group Negativity
- Post-acute Withdrawal
- Resistance Based on Distorted Beliefs about Substance Abuse/Dependence
- Shame Issues
- Substance Abuse
- Substance Dependence
- Substance Withdrawal
- Tendency to Repeated Relapse
- Treatment/Aftercare Noncompliance

2

SUGGESTIONS FOR PROCESSING THIS EXERCISE WITH CLIENT

1. How have your thoughts changed regarding abuse and addiction?
2. How will this new insight assist you in making decisions related to the use of alcohol or other drugs?
3. How does this information about how substance abuse and addiction work change your views and expectations of yourself?

WHAT DOES ABUSE/ ADDICTION MEAN TO ME?

It is important for you to identify patterns of using and how your life events fit these patterns. This exercise will help you do so.

1. For each of the following symptoms, please write about whether this has happened in your life, and if it has, give an example.

    a. Tolerance (needing more of a chemical to get the same desired effect, or feeling less effect with the same amount):

    _____

    _____

    b. Withdrawal (either experiencing withdrawal symptoms after stopping use, or using or drinking to relieve or avoid withdrawal symptoms):

    _____

    _____

    c. Loss of control (using/drinking in larger amounts or for longer periods of time than you intended):

    _____

    _____

    d. Attempts to control use (having a persistent desire or making efforts to control or cut down on your using/drinking, including making rules or bargains with yourself to limit it):

    _____

    _____

    e. Time spent on use (getting the chemical, using it, or recovering from its effects):

    _____

    _____

4

f. Sacrifices made for use (giving up or reducing social, work, family, or recreational activities that were important to you because using/drinking interfered with them):

_____

_____

g. Use despite known suffering (continuing to use/drink despite knowing you had a physical or psychological problem that was caused or made worse by using/drinking):

_____

_____

2. Looking back over these symptoms, what do they tell you about your use of substances?

_____

_____

_____

_____

3. For each of the following stages of drinking or drug use, please note whether you have experienced this, and if you have, give an example of how your life fits the description.

a. First stage: First experience, when people begin using a chemical and discover that they like the way the chemical makes them feel:

_____

_____

_____

b. Second stage: Tolerance and withdrawal appear, and people find that they can use the chemical to cope with situations or feelings that are difficult or uncomfortable:

_____

_____

_____

c. Third stage: People begin deliberately using the chemical to cope, and may try to cut down or control use; their normal life is disrupted and others start believing there's a problem:

_____

_____

_____

d. Fourth stage: People feel that they cannot cope without the chemical and will pay whatever price comes with continued use; they feel a conflict between wanting to use versus not wanting to use; they feel trapped; life seems to be falling apart:

_____

_____

_____

4. Looking over these four phases of developing chemical dependence, what have you learned about your own pattern of use?

_____

_____

_____

Remember to bring completed work sheet to your next appointment.

Problem Identification

GOALS OF THE EXERCISE

1. To assist clients in increasing their awareness of losses and problems associated with their use of alcohol and other drugs.
2. To increase readiness for change to avoid further problems brought on by or made worse by use of alcohol or other drugs.
3. To help clients become aware that there are self-destructive behaviors associated with their use of alcohol or other drugs; to personalize the effects on their lives.
4. To provide objective data about the impact of alcohol or other drug use or dependence.

TYPES OF PROBLEMS THIS EXERCISE MAY BE MOST USEFUL FOR

- Blaming/Projection/Failure to Take Appropriate Responsibility
- Denial/Rationalization/Minimization of Substance-Abusing Behavior and/or Relapse Risk
- Family Conflict
- General Interpersonal Relational Problems
- Generalized Treatment Resistance
- History of Self-Medication for Mood/Pain Problems
- Learned Helplessness
- Living Environment Deficiencies (Relapse Triggers, Lack of Emotional Support, etc.)
- Low Self-Esteem
- Peer Group Negativity
- Post-acute Withdrawal
- Resistance Based on Distorted Beliefs about Substance Abuse/Dependence
- Shame Issues
- Substance Abuse
- Substance Dependence

- Substance Withdrawal
- Tendency to Repeated Relapse
- Treatment/Aftercare Noncompliance

SUGGESTIONS FOR PROCESSING THIS EXERCISE WITH CLIENT

1. What did you learn about your own level of use/abuse/dependence and life problems associated with use?
2. Do you see possible connections between problems that you thought were unrelated? If so, does this give you more hope of solving several other problems by working on this one?

PROBLEM IDENTIFICATION

People don't usually seek treatment or help until something forces them to ask themselves, "What got me here?"—in other words, until they encounter some kind of crisis. Crises are good motivators, but they go away, and people need to make decisions about using that will to carry them beyond the crisis. If you wonder whether you have a problem with alcohol or other drugs or how serious your problem is, compare the events in your life with each of the following categories.

1. Here is a brief list of common experiences that bring people who are using alcohol or other drugs to decide that they should stop their use of these substances, that their drinking or drug use is causing them problems, and that they need help. Check all that apply to you:

Loss of Important Relationships because of Drinking/Using

__ Divorce or equivalent

__ Loss of close friendships

__ Alienation of children, parents, siblings

__ Loss of respect from coworkers

Practical Difficulties Resulting from Drinking/Using

__ Unpayable debts

__ Loss of a home

__ Loss of a vehicle

__ Legal problems (*arrest, jail, probation, loss of driver's license, etc.*)

__ Loss of employment

__ Loss of professional status

Dangerous/Harmful Situations Resulting from Drinking/Using

__ Health problems

__ Work injuries, falls, or other accidents

__ Harm to others as a result of one's own actions under the influence

__ DUIs, DWIs, or car wrecks

__ Recreational accidents

__ Fights while under the influence or coming down

9

Things You Once Thought You'd Never Do

__ Lying to partners/families   __ Stealing from partners/families

__ Abandoning partners/families   __ Endangering others, especially children

__ Breaking promises   __ Letting down friends

__ Abusing family members   __ Exchanging sex for drugs or alcohol

__ Letting down employers   __ Selling drugs

__ Committing crimes for
      substances

2. When you think, or thought in the past, about your life without alcohol or other drugs, what types of feelings do you or did you experience?

_____

_____

3. Do you see any other evidence that your use of alcohol or of other drugs is causing problems in your life? If you do, what is it?

_____

_____

Remember to bring completed work sheet to your next appointment.

Where Am I?

GOALS OF THE EXERCISE

1. To normalize common stresses and changes newly sober people experience.
2. To assist clients in assessing what they are currently experiencing and give them some idea of what feelings, thoughts, and events they may experience during the process of change.
3. To help clients identify reasons why making changes will benefit them.

TYPES OF PROBLEMS THIS EXERCISE MAY BE MOST USEFUL FOR

- Anger Management
- Anxiety
- Appetite Disturbance
- Burnout
- Codependency
- Denial/Rationalization/Minimization of Substance-Abusing Behavior and/or Relapse Risk
- Depression
- Emotional Isolation
- General Interpersonal Relational Problems
- Generalized Treatment Resistance
- Hopelessness
- Inadequate Support Network
- Legal Problems
- Learned Helplessness
- Living Environment Deficiencies (Relapse Triggers, Lack of Emotional Support, etc.)
- Low Self-Esteem
- Mood Swings
- Peer Group Negativity

- Post-acute Withdrawal
- Resistance Based on Distorted Beliefs about Substance Abuse/Dependence
- Shame Issues
- Sleep Disturbance
- Substance Abuse
- Substance Dependence
- Substance Withdrawal
- Tendency to Repeated Relapse
- Treatment/Aftercare Noncompliance

SUGGESTIONS FOR PROCESSING THIS EXERCISE WITH CLIENT

1. How will you cope with events that may happen as you continue in a nonusing lifestyle?
2. What events are you prepared to deal with?
3. Where might you need some assistance and where will you find it?
4. Ask about the client's exercise in imagination from the end of the assignment.

WHERE AM I?

There are common patterns of events, thoughts, and feelings that newly sober people often experience as they change to a lifestyle that does not involve using alcohol or other drugs or engaging in other compulsive behaviors. This exercise will help you identify where you are in this process and what your current level of motivation is.

1. Following is a list of common events people experience. For each of the following, please write about whether this is happening or has happened to you, and if it has, give an example.

    a. Feeling physical changes in your body as it becomes free of alcohol/other drugs:

    _____

    _____

    b. Feelings of hope and exhilaration: _____

    _____

    c. Feelings of letdown and fear: _____

    _____

    d. Frustration: _____

    _____

    e. Feeling more connected to other people: _____

    _____

    f. Loneliness:_____

    _____

    g. Feeling strange or out of place:_____

    _____

    h. Ongoing cravings, urges, thoughts of using/drinking: _____

    _____

i. Feeling doubtful or questioning self, spirituality, values, abilities: _____

_____

j. Mood fluctuations: _____

_____

2.   The reason I decided to get clean and sober now is: _____

_____

3.   I want to change these things about my life: _____

_____

_____

4.   Now we ask you to do an exercise in imagination: Picture yourself in the future, living a life free of any drug or harmful behavior you have been depending on. What alternative ways are you using in this life to react to difficult situations and uncomfortable feelings? As you picture yourself living this way, how does that image of yourself make you feel?

_____

_____

Remember to bring completed work sheet to your next appointment.

Understanding Family History

GOALS OF THE EXERCISE

1. To examine the influence of the client's family of origin in the development and maintenance of substance-abusing behaviors and recovery.
2. To help the client to learn new ways to interact with his or her own family.
3. To help the client see that he or she can learn from the experiences of others.

TYPES OF PROBLEMS THIS EXERCISE MAY BE MOST USEFUL FOR

- Adult Children of Alcoholic (ACOA) Traits
- Anger Management
- Blaming/Projection/Failure to Take Appropriate Responsibility
- Borderline Traits
- Codependency
- Denial/Rationalization/Minimization of Substance-Abusing Behavior and/or Relapse Risk
- Depression
- Emotional Isolation
- Family Conflict
- General Interpersonal Relational Problems
- Inadequate Support Network
- Issues of Identity
- Learned Helplessness
- Living Environment Deficiencies (Relapse Triggers, Lack of Emotional Support, etc.)
- Low Self-Esteem
- Parent-Child Relational Problems
- Partner Relational Problems
- Poor Social Skills
- Posttraumatic Stress Issues

- Shame Issues
- Substance Abuse
- Substance Dependence
- Unresolved Childhood Trauma
- Unresolved Grief and Loss

SUGGESTIONS FOR PROCESSING THIS EXERCISE WITH CLIENT

1. What patterns do you see being repeated, generation after generation, in your family or in other families you know?
2. Does this exercise cause you to think of any of your own experiences in a different way? If so, what is the change?
3. Do you see patterns in your own life you want to avoid passing on to your children?
4. What new pattern would you want to replace an old pattern in your family and your life?

UNDERSTANDING FAMILY HISTORY

It's important to understand the role family history can play in the development of substance abuse or chemical dependence, both for your own recovery and to improve things for your family. Biological, psychological, and social factors combine in different ways for different people to influence the development of substance abuse. This exercise looks at one of these factors: the way social influences affect us.

1. Who did you see drinking or using in your family of origin? What age were you? What effects do you believe this had on you?

    _____

    _____

2. What did you learn about alcohol or other drugs from your family of origin?

    _____

    _____

3. What problems, if any, did your family have as a result of drinking or using (violence, divorce, financial problems, other worries, illegal activity)?

    _____

    _____

4. What chemicals and how much were you or others in your family using?

    _____

5. What words best describe the typical atmosphere or mood in your family of origin?

    _____

6. Members of alcohol- or drug-using families often interact with each other in some common patterns. For each pattern listed here that you experienced, give an example from childhood and an example of how you are working to make positive changes in your family now.

Dishonesty/denial

Childhood example: _____

Working toward positive change: _____

Breaking promises

Childhood example: _____

Working toward positive change: _____

Isolating/withdrawing

Childhood example: _____

Working toward positive change: _____

Emotional/physical/sexual abuse and neglect

Childhood example: _____

Working toward positive change: _____

Influencing others to act in self-destructive ways

Childhood example: _____

Working toward positive change: _____

Inappropriate role assignment (such as children taking caring of adults)

Childhood example: _____

Working toward positive change: _____

Taking responsibility for others/expecting others to take responsibility for you

Childhood example: _____

Working toward positive change: _____

7. Are there any relationship patterns from your childhood family that you feel were good and want to pass on to your children? If so, what are they?

_____

_____

8. How does your family of origin still impact your use of alcohol or other drugs, ineffective or self-harming behavior, or recovery efforts?

    _____

    _____

9. What questions do you want to ask the group or therapist about this topic in your next session?

    _____

    _____

    _____

    _____

Remember to bring completed work sheet to your next appointment.

Identifying Social/Cultural Influences and Pressures to Drink/Use

GOALS OF THE EXERCISE

1. To increase the client's understanding of pressures to drink or use so that he or she will be more capable of resisting these pressures.
2. To suggest that the client can take actions to reach the goal of abstinence, despite pressures from the social environment.

TYPES OF PROBLEMS THIS EXERCISE MAY BE MOST USEFUL FOR

- Blaming/Projection/Failure to Take Appropriate Responsibility
- Denial/Rationalization/Minimization of Substance-Abusing Behavior and/or Relapse Risk
- Inadequate Support Network
- Living Environment Deficiencies (Relapse Triggers, Lack of Emotional Support, etc.)
- Peer Group Negativity
- Spiritual Confusion
- Substance Abuse
- Substance Dependence
- Tendency to Repeated Relapse
- Treatment/Aftercare Noncompliance
- Value Conflicts

SUGGESTIONS FOR PROCESSING THIS EXERCISE WITH CLIENT

1. Role-play different pressure situations in individual sessions or groups.
2. What is the biggest obstacle for you in resisting pressure to return to using/drinking?
3. Rehearse what you will say to people who may pressure you if you encounter them.

IDENTIFYING SOCIAL/CULTURAL INFLUENCES AND PRESSURES TO DRINK/USE

Knowing how to identify pressures toward relapse, and knowing what to do and what not to do, is not only helpful but necessary to prevent returning to use of alcohol or other drugs. This knowledge will help you handle pressures you may have been unable to resist before. Some social and cultural pressures are easy to identify, though they may be either easy or hard to resist. This exercise will help you identify your personal pressures and develop a plan to cope with them.

1. Below are some sources of social or cultural pressures to drink or use. Please give an example of how each might be a source of social pressure to drink or use for you.

    a. Family members: _____

    b. Friends, peers: _____

    c. Recreational activities: _____

    d. Celebrations (religious, cultural, family, etc.): _____

    e. Work environment: _____

2. Identify one action you will take to resist each pressure you identified.

    a. Family members: _____

    b. Friends, peers: _____

    c. Recreational activities: _____

    d. Celebrations: _____

    e. Work environment: _____

3. Mental rehearsal: Try to act these strategies out in your mind. Picture what you will be doing and saying. Then answer these questions.

    a. What problems did you foresee when you tried to imagine doing this? _____

    _____

b. What went right? _____
_____

c. What skills do you need to learn in order to succeed in resisting social pressures to use? _____
_____
_____

Remember to bring completed work sheet to your next appointment.

Section II

Identifying Goals and Motivation for Recovery

What Would My Ideal Life Look Like?

GOALS OF THE EXERCISE

1. To help the client clarify and prioritize life values and goals.
2. To increase the client's awareness of ways in which substance abuse interferes with achieving values and goals.
3. To strengthen the client's motivation for treatment by identifying benefits achievable in recovery.

TYPES OF PROBLEMS THIS EXERCISE MAY BE MOST USEFUL FOR

*   General Interpersonal Relational Problems
*   Issues of Identity
*   Learned Helplessness
*   Low Self-Esteem
*   Occupational Problems
*   Parent-Child Relational Problems
*   Partner Relational Problems
*   Shame Issues
*   Spiritual Confusion
*   Value Conflicts

SUGGESTIONS FOR PROCESSING THIS
EXERCISE WITH CLIENT

1. What was the first thing you thought of when you started this exercise?
2. How much difference will being clean and sober make in your ability to achieve your ideal life?
3. Will being abstinent from alcohol, other drugs, or addictive behaviors interfere with achieving your ideal life?
4. Have you found your ideas about what would make you happy changing while you've worked on your recovery? If so, what has changed?

WHAT WOULD MY IDEAL LIFE LOOK LIKE?

This assignment is designed to strengthen your motivation for recovery by helping you identify the benefits of sobriety that will mean the most to you personally. It should also help you set some goals above and beyond recovery and focus on what changes in your life would make you happiest and give you the most fulfillment.

1. Do you have a clear idea of what your ideal life would be like? Please think about this for a moment, then fill in the following sections with short descriptions of your ideal life in each area.

   a. Where would you live? _____

   _____

   b. What would your marital/family situation be? _____

   _____

   _____

   c. What would your work be? _____

   _____

   d. What would be your proudest achievements?_____

   _____

   _____

   e. What would your hobbies and leisure activities be?_____

   _____

   _____

   f. How would other people think of you? _____

   _____

   _____

2. Now, let's see what it would take to get from where you are today to where you want to be.

    a. Where would you live?

    Situation now   *Ideal situation*   *What change is needed?*

    _____   _____   _____
    _____   _____   _____
    _____   _____   _____

    b. What would your marital/family situation be?

    Situation now   *Ideal situation*   *What change is needed?*

    _____   _____   _____
    _____   _____   _____
    _____   _____   _____

    c. What would your work be?

    Situation now   *Ideal situation*   *What change is needed?*

    _____   _____   _____
    _____   _____   _____
    _____   _____   _____

    d. What would be your proudest achievements?

    Situation now   *Ideal situation*   *What change is needed?*

    _____   _____   _____
    _____   _____   _____
    _____   _____   _____

    e. What would your hobbies and leisure activities be?

    Situation now   *Ideal situation*   *What change is needed?*

    _____   _____   _____
    _____   _____   _____
    _____   _____   _____

f. How would other people think of you?

Situation now   *Ideal situation*   *What change is needed?*

_____   _____   _____

_____   _____   _____

_____   _____   _____

3. Concentrating on the changes needed, please consider the impact of abusing alcohol or other drugs on your chances of making the changes you want.

	Drinking/using will help	*Drinking/using will interfere*	*No difference either way*
a. Where you would live	____	____	____
b. Marital/family situation	____	____	____
c. Work situation	____	____	____
d. Hobbies/leisure	____	____	____
e. What others think	____	____	____
Total	____	____	____

4. This time, let's look at the effects of being clean and sober.

	Sobriety will help	*Sobriety will interfere*	*No difference either way*
a. Where you would live	____	____	____
b. Marital/family situation	____	____	____
c. Work situation	____	____	____
d. Hobbies/leisure	____	____	____
e. What others think	____	____	____
Total	____	____	____

5. Some final questions—please write your answers, and feel free to add comments beyond "yes" or "no."

a. If you see that drinking or using will interfere with your chances of achieving your most cherished dreams, but you keep on drinking or using anyway, aren't your actions showing that alcohol or another drug is actually more important to you than those dreams?

_____

_____

_____

_____

_____

b. If someone you knew put drinking or using other drugs ahead of his or her dreams and ideals, would you think that he or she had a substance abuse problem? Would you think it meant he or she was an alcoholic or addict?

_____

_____

_____

_____

_____

c. If this is happening in your life, do you suppose the people who know you would say you had a problem? _____ If you feel you don't, how do you explain this conflict between values and actions?

_____

_____

_____

_____

_____

Remember to bring completed work sheet to your next appointment.

What Did I Want to Be When I Grew Up?

GOALS OF THE EXERCISE

1. To help the client identify the impact of substance abuse on achievement of life goals.
2. To increase the client's experience of cognitive dissonance by comparing a substance-abusing lifestyle with his or her childhood ambitions.
3. To strengthen the client's motivation for treatment by helping him or her reconnect with old ideals and dreams.

TYPES OF PROBLEMS THIS EXERCISE MAY BE MOST USEFUL FOR

- Adult Children of Alcoholic (ACOA) Traits
- Depression
- Hopelessness
- Issues of Identity
- Learned Helplessness
- Low Self-Esteem
- Occupational Problems
- Spiritual Confusion
- Tendency to Repeated Relapse
- Unresolved Childhood Trauma
- Value Conflicts

SUGGESTIONS FOR PROCESSING THIS EXERCISE WITH CLIENT

1. What was the first thing you thought of when you started this exercise?
2. Do you still feel you'd like to live those childhood dreams?
3. Does using alcohol or other drugs, or addictive behavior, fit with your childhood dreams?
4. Would being abstinent from alcohol, other drugs, or addictive behaviors fit with your childhood dreams?

WHAT DID I WANT TO BE
WHEN I GREW UP?

> *This assignment is designed to strengthen your motivation for recovery by helping you reconnect with early dreams and ideals you may not have thought about for a long time. Although we often put childhood dreams aside in adulthood, those daydreaming children are still a part of our inner selves, and can tell us a lot about our true identity and nature.*

1. Take a moment to think back to your childhood. What is the first memory you have of wanting to do a certain job or play a certain role when you grew up—how old were you, and what did you want to do or be?

   _____

   _____

2. What other jobs or roles did you dream about as you grew older?

   _____

   _____

3. What does your life now have in common with the life you dreamed about as a child or teen?

   _____

   _____

4. Whether they are practical or not, do your youthful dreams still appeal to you? _____ If they do, are there things you can do as an adult that would be like those dreams in some way? For example, a child who dreamed of being an explorer could be an investigative reporter or a research scientist. What are some things you can do that are in the same spirit as those dreams?

   _____

   _____

5. When you thought about your future while you were growing up, did you think about using alcohol or other drugs in that future? If you did, how did you picture yourself drinking or using?

_____

_____

6. If you had been able to see the future when you were a child, and had seen the role alcohol or other drugs would play in your life, what would you have thought?

_____

_____

_____

_____

7. Now do an exercise in imagination. Find a quiet place where you can do some thinking without being disturbed for a while. Sit in a comfortable position. Close your eyes, and picture yourself at the happiest time of your childhood, whatever age you were then. Now picture the child you were, standing in front of you looking at you. As you picture this child meeting the adult version of you, what expression is on his or her face? Think about what you would say to that child, what you would want him or her to know about you.

   Now put yourself in that child's shoes. Look at the adult sitting in front of you. What would you, as your childhood self, want to say to this person? What would you ask him or her? Imagine yourself, as the child, telling your adult self about your hopes and dreams. What answer do you think this adult would give you?

   Continue the exercise in imagination. Picture the adult you are now, going through your typical day, accompanied by the child you were. Which parts of your day would you be proud to have that child watch? Are there parts of your day, parts of your life, you would rather that child didn't see? If so, why do you feel that way?

   As part of your therapy, you can talk with your therapist about this exercise and what it is like for you. You might find it helps you strengthen your connections to your oldest, strongest ideals and dreams to make this exercise a part of your daily or weekly routine, spending time with your inner child regularly.

Remember to bring completed work sheet to your next appointment.

What Do I Want for My Children?

GOALS OF THE EXERCISE

1. To help the client identify the impact of substance abuse on his or her children.
2. To increase the client's experience of cognitive dissonance by comparing how he or she wants to function as a parent with the changes substance abuse causes in parents and families.
3. To strengthen the client's motivation for treatment by helping him or her compare his or her own childhood experiences with those he or she is passing on to the next generation.

TYPES OF PROBLEMS THIS EXERCISE MAY BE MOST USEFUL FOR

- Adult Children of Alcoholic (ACOA) Traits
- Anger Management
- Antisocial Behavior
- Blaming/Projection/Failure to Take Appropriate Responsibility
- Borderline Traits
- Codependency
- Denial/Rationalization/Minimization of Substance-Abusing Behavior and/or Relapse Risk
- Family Conflict
- Issues of Identity
- Narcissistic Traits
- Parent-Child Relational Problems
- Spiritual Confusion
- Substance Abuse
- Substance Dependence
- Tendency to Repeated Relapse
- Treatment/Aftercare Noncompliance

- Unresolved Childhood Trauma
- Value Conflicts

SUGGESTIONS FOR PROCESSING THIS EXERCISE WITH CLIENT

1. What was the first thing you thought of when you heard the title of this exercise?
2. Do you feel your use of alcohol or other drugs has affected your performance of your role as a parent?
3. In what ways do you see yourself recreating your own childhood experiences in the lives of your children? How do you feel about that?
4. In what ways are you making your children's lives different from what you experienced at the same ages? How do you feel about that?

WHAT DO I WANT FOR MY CHILDREN?

> *This assignment is designed to strengthen your motivation for recovery by helping you focus on how you affect your children's lives, both positively and negatively (and we all do both). It may prompt you to take a fresh look at your family life and how it is affected by drinking, using, or other addictive behaviors.*

1. Think back to your childhood. All of us looked at some of the things our parents (or whoever raised us) did and told ourselves, "I want to do the same thing with my children someday." All of us also looked at some of the actions of the adults in our lives and promised ourselves, "I'm never going to do that with my kids." Please take a few minutes to list your personal top five items in each category.

    a. "I want to do this with my children someday."

    _____

    _____

    _____

    _____

    _____

    b. "I'll never do that with my kids!"

    _____

    _____

    _____

    _____

    _____

2. Now leap forward in time to the day you first found out you were going to be a parent—or, if you don't have children, to your thoughts on how you would want to act as a parent if you had children. List your top five goals in adulthood for things you do and don't want to do with your children.

a. "I want to do this with my children someday."

_____
_____
_____
_____
_____

b. "I'll never do that with my kids!"

_____
_____
_____
_____
_____

3. As a child, were you strongly affected by the drinking or drug use of one or both of your parents, or of some other adult who played an important role in your life? _____ Please write briefly about what happened and how you felt about it then.

_____
_____
_____

4. Was this experience one you would choose to pass on to your own children? _____

5. Please list any of your goals as a parent, present or future, that you feel would be helped by your drinking or drug use.

_____
_____
_____

6. Now list any parental goals you have that drinking or using might interfere with.

_____
_____
_____
_____

7. If you see that drinking or using will interfere with your chances of giving your children the kind of childhood you want them to have, but you keep on drinking or using anyway, aren't your actions showing that alcohol or another drug is actually more important to you than your children? _____ What is your plan to deal with this? _____

    _____

8. If someone you knew put drinking or using other drugs ahead of his or her ability to do his or her best as a parent, would you think he or she had a substance abuse problem? Would you think it meant he or she was an alcoholic or addict?

9. If this is happening in your life, do you suppose your children would say you had a problem? _____ If you feel you don't have a problem, how would you explain this conflict between values and actions to your children if they asked?

    _____

    _____

    _____

    _____

    _____

    _____

Remember to bring completed work sheet to your next appointment.

What Price Am I Willing to Pay? Examining Consequences and Identifying My "Bottom"

GOALS OF THE EXERCISE

1. To help the client identify the impact of substance abuse on his or her life.
2. To increase the client's experience of cognitive dissonance by comparing his or her stated values with the actions and experiences inherent in a substance-abusing lifestyle.
3. To help the client establish his or her standards for a threshold level of substance abuse that would convince him or her that alcohol or other drugs have become an unacceptable problem.

TYPES OF PROBLEMS THIS EXERCISE MAY BE MOST USEFUL FOR

- Anger Management
- Antisocial Behavior
- Blaming/Projection/Failure to Take Appropriate Responsibility
- Denial/Rationalization/Minimization of Substance-Abusing Behavior and/or Relapse Risk
- Generalized Treatment Resistance
- Grandiosity
- Impulsivity
- Issues of Identity
- Legal Problems
- Learned Helplessness
- Mania/Hypomania
- Medical Issues
- Narcissistic Traits
- Occupational Problems
- Parent-Child Relational Problems
- Partner Relational Problems
- Resistance Based on Distorted Beliefs about Substance Abuse/Dependence

- Spiritual Confusion
- Substance Abuse
- Substance Dependence
- Tendency to Repeated Relapse
- Treatment/Aftercare Noncompliance
- Value Conflicts

SUGGESTIONS FOR PROCESSING THIS EXERCISE WITH CLIENT

1. When you heard the title of this exercise, what mental picture did you get of prices you may have paid or of what would be the bottom for you?
2. Have you done things you thought you would never do while you were drinking or using? What was that like?
3. Did you have a clear understanding of what consequences of substance abuse you would find unacceptable before you did this exercise? When you finished, had your views on this changed? If so, how?
4. What experiences have you seen other people go through that would make you feel you needed to give up alcohol or other drugs?

WHAT PRICE AM I WILLING TO PAY? EXAMINING CONSEQUENCES AND IDENTIFYING MY "BOTTOM"

> *This assignment is designed to help you clarify your own beliefs about what consequences of substance abuse would be so unacceptable to you that you would feel you had to avoid them at any cost, even if that meant permanently giving up alcohol or other drugs.*

1. You may have heard someone say that for an alcoholic or addict to give up drinking and drug use, he or she has to hit bottom. What does hitting bottom mean to you?

   _____

   _____

   _____

   _____

   _____

2. While some may think that hitting bottom means becoming homeless or some other very drastic consequence of substance use, it may not mean that at all for many people. In fact, each of us has a bottom level that is unique to us; used this way, the word merely means that we experience something we find so unacceptable that we just can't let it happen—or let it happen again—no matter what. Some people have higher bottom levels than others, simply because they are willing to suffer less. With this in mind, think about your own bottom level and answer these questions:

   a. Have you seen someone else experience a consequence of substance use that you felt you could not have tolerated in your own life? If so, what was it?

   _____

   _____

   b. Have you ever promised yourself you would quit drinking or using if a particular thing happened in your life because of your substance use? _____ If you have, what was the experience you told yourself you couldn't tolerate?

   _____

   _____

3. What negative consequences have you experienced? Check any that have happened to you. Circle any you've experienced more than once and write the number of times.

___ Spent money on drinking/using that you needed for something else

___ Been embarrassed by what you said or did while under the influence

___ Gotten sick in public

___ Driven while under the influence

___ Experienced physical withdrawal

___ Experienced increased tolerance

___ Drunk/used more than you meant to

___ Been asked to quit by others

___ Lied about your drinking/drug use

___ Experienced an overdose

___ Gone to work under the influence

___ Embarrassed members of your family

___ Passed out due to drinking/using

___ Experienced blackouts (memory gaps)

___ Been arrested for DUI/DWI

___ Lost a job due to drinking/using

___ Alienated yourself from friends/relatives

___ Been divorced due to drinking/using

___ Gotten in a fight while under the influence

___ Had a car accident while drinking/using

___ Hurt someone else due to drinking/using

___ Hoarded alcohol or other drugs

___ Gotten hurt in a sports/recreational accident while drinking/using

___ Been unfaithful to your partner while drinking/using

___ Hidden your alcohol or other drugs from family or friends

___ Sold or traded possessions to get alcohol or other drugs

___ Avoided an activity because it interfered with drinking/using

___ Committed a crime while drinking/using

___ Committed a crime to get alcohol or another drug

___ Been in jail or prison due to drinking/using

___ Traded sex for alcohol or other drugs

___ Sold illegal drugs to buy more drugs

___ Considered suicide while drinking/using or due to consequences of drinking/using

___ Attempted suicide while drinking/using

___ Accidentally killed someone while drinking/using

___ Intentionally killed someone while drinking/using

4. Now look back over Question 3, which you just finished. Have you experienced any of the negative consequences you once said would be unacceptable to you (see Question 2)? _____ Which one(s)?

_____

_____

5. Now refer to Question 3 again, and list all the items you have experienced, with the number of times for items you have experienced more than once.

_____

_____

_____

_____

6. Picture yourself talking with a close friend, or perhaps a brother or sister, and hearing him or her tell you about experiencing all the consequences listed in your answer for Question 5. Picture this person asking your advice about his or her use of alcohol or other drugs. Would you be worried about this friend's drinking/using? _____ Would you feel that this was such a serious problem that it would be best for the person to quit completely? _____ What would you say to your friend or relative about this?

_____

_____

7. Are there consequences listed in Question 3 that you may have experienced once, but that you would feel meant your drinking or drug use was out of control if they happened again? Which ones?

_____

_____

8. Are there consequences listed in Question 3 that you have never experienced that would be a bottom for you—that is, would signal you that you needed to quit permanently? Which ones?

_____

_____

43

9. Now go back to Question 3, and list any of the consequences you have experienced that you do not consider unpleasant or serious enough to lead you to quit drinking or using.

    _____

    _____

    _____

10. Review the items you just listed. *By saying that you have experienced these but do not feel they are bad enough to make you quit drinking or using, you are saying that going without your drug of choice would be worse for you than those consequences.* Think about your relationship with alcohol or whatever drug(s) you have preferred. If you heard someone else say that living without a drug would be a greater loss than these consequences, what would you think about that person's use of that chemical?

    _____

    _____

11. After working through this assignment, you may have a clearer idea of where your bottom level is when it comes to substance use, and you may also have changed some of your thinking about the role alcohol or another drug has played in your life.

    a. Please use this space to write about any changes in your views on your own drinking or drug use.

        _____

        _____

    b. Describe what you think of as your bottom level—the consequences you could not accept.

        _____

        _____

    c. Now describe what you will do if you experience one of the consequences you have decided would be your bottom level. If this happens, what action will you take?

        _____

        _____

Remember to bring completed work sheet to your next appointment.

Making a Yet List: Consequences of Continuing Addictive Lifestyles

GOALS OF THE EXERCISE

1. To help the client clarify the limits of the negative consequences of substance abuse he or she is willing to tolerate without quitting.
2. To focus the client's attention on the negative consequences he or she and others experience due to drinking and use of drugs.

TYPES OF PROBLEMS THIS EXERCISE MAY BE MOST USEFUL FOR

- Anger Management
- Antisocial Behavior
- Blaming/Projection/Failure to Take Appropriate Responsibility
- Denial/Rationalization/Minimization of Substance-Abusing Behavior and/or Relapse Risk
- Family Conflict
- General Interpersonal Relational Problems
- Generalized Treatment Resistance
- Grandiosity
- Impulsivity
- Legal Problems
- Mania/Hypomania
- Medical Issues
- Narcissistic Traits
- Occupational Problems
- Parent-Child Relational Problems
- Partner Relational Problems
- Peer Group Negativity
- Spiritual Confusion
- Substance Abuse

- Substance Dependence
- Tendency to Repeated Relapse
- Treatment/Aftercare Noncompliance
- Value Conflicts

SUGGESTIONS FOR PROCESSING THIS EXERCISE WITH CLIENT

1. What was the first consequence of drinking or using that you thought of when you understood what this exercise is about?
2. What is it about the experiences you have decided you could not tolerate that makes them unacceptable for you? Is there a common thread tying them together?
3. Think of some aspect of your life that you value, such as a hobby or a friendship with another person. If you began experiencing negative consequences because of that activity or relationship, how bad would they have to get before you decided to give up the activity or relationship? Is your bottom level with your drug of choice more or less unpleasant than it would be for this other part of your life? What does that tell you?

MAKING A YET LIST: CONSEQUENCES OF CONTINUING ADDICTIVE LIFESTYLES

This assignment is designed to help you see more clearly what your limits are when it comes to suffering negative consequences of substance abuse. Once you've finished this, it would probably be helpful to talk about it with your therapist and/or program sponsor.

1. Have you ever made a yet list before, or heard of the idea? _____ When you hear the words, what thoughts go through your mind?

    _____

    _____

2. A yet list is merely a list of the negative consequences of substance abuse that you know could happen, but that you have not experienced yet. What use would a list like this be to people dealing with alcohol and other drug problems?

    _____

    _____

3. As you may have heard or figured out, a yet list is used to create your personal definition of being out of control. This is a list of experiences you feel would show you that you needed to quit drinking or using. First, do you agree that if you truly believed your drinking or drug use was out of control, you would need to quit? _____ Why or why not?

    _____

    _____

    _____

4. Now make your list: First, write down here (or, if you are working with a group, on a plain piece of paper, chalkboard, or something else everyone can see) all the negative consequences of drinking and using drugs other than alcohol *that you have never experienced* that you can think of. If you have a group to work with, having everyone brainstorm on this for a few minutes is a good way to get a longer list of consequences.

    _____

    _____

    _____

_____

_____

_____

5. Now look at this list. Which of these experiences have you escaped through luck (for example, driving under the influence and escaping arrest because you missed a sobriety checkpoint)?

_____

_____

_____

_____

6. Which experiences have you never been in danger of having happen in your life? (For example, if you never drive under the influence, you've never been in danger of arrest for DWI.) Which of these are likely to happen if you keep on drinking or using?

_____

_____

_____

_____

_____

7. Which experiences from your list of things that haven't yet happened to you would you personally consider to be definite evidence that your drinking or drug use was unsafe or out of control?

_____

_____

_____

_____

_____

8. The experiences you listed for Question 7 are your yet list, because they've happened to others who drank and used but haven't happened to you *yet*. Since these are things you have decided would show that your drinking or using was out of control, what will you do if one of them does happen to you?

_____

_____

9. If you truly feel that the items on your yet list are unacceptable and would mean you had to quit drinking or using, how do you plan to do so if one of them happens?

    _____

    _____

10. How can your family, your friends, your therapist, your coworkers, and others you know in some way help you make the commitment to seek help in quitting alcohol or other drugs if you experience one or more of the events on your yet list?

    _____

    _____

    _____

    _____

11. If you are willing to make a formal commitment to follow through on the decision you talked about in Question 7, how can others help you carry that decision out? What would it help you for them to do?

    _____

    _____

    _____

    _____

12. Who can help you with this? It's a good idea to talk to these people ahead of time, while you're clean, sober, and hopefully calm and rational, and explain what you are asking them to do for you. We suggest specifically asking them how they would feel if you came to them for help.

    Remember to bring completed work sheet to your next appointment.

Section III

Identifying Strengths, Resources, and Methods

What Already Works?
Identifying Proven Problem-Solving
Skills and Strengths

GOALS OF THE EXERCISE

1. To help the client clarify and effectively use innate strengths and resources in his or her community and environment.
2. To reframe recovery from addiction as a problem to be solved, having much in common with other problems the client has already solved.
3. To strengthen the client's motivation for treatment by identifying recovery tools he or she has been using since childhood.

TYPES OF PROBLEMS THIS EXERCISE MAY
BE MOST USEFUL FOR

*   Anxiety
*   Borderline Traits
*   Depression
*   Emotional Isolation
*   Hopelessness
*   Inadequate Support Network
*   Legal Problems
*   Learned Helplessness
*   Living Environment Deficiencies (Relapse Triggers, Lack of Emotional Support, etc.)
*   Low Self-Esteem
*   Medical Issues
*   Mood Swings
*   Occupational Problems
*   Parent-Child Relational Problems
*   Partner Relational Problems
*   Peer Group Negativity
*   Poor Social Skills

- Post-acute Withdrawal
- Posttraumatic Stress Issues
- Shame Issues
- Substance Abuse
- Substance Dependence
- Tendency to Repeated Relapse

SUGGESTIONS FOR PROCESSING THIS EXERCISE WITH CLIENT

1. What kinds of problems and challenges are you most successful at overcoming?
2. If you could handle problems while you were drinking or using, how much better can you handle them unimpaired?
3. Which skills and traits describe you the best? Can you give some examples?

WHAT ALREADY WORKS? IDENTIFYING PROVEN PROBLEM-SOLVING SKILLS AND STRENGTHS

This assignment is designed to strengthen your recovery program quickly by helping you find ways to apply skills and qualities you already have. Everyone has problem-solving methods they have used in other situations, and we each have a unique combination of talents. In this exercise you will look at your past successes in all areas of life to find recovery tools you already have.

1.   Often, when a person enters a drug or alcohol treatment program, he or she hears a lot of terms being used in what may be unfamiliar ways. Staff and more experienced clients use terms like *sharing, dependence, abstinence, surrender, denial, recovery, Higher Power,* and others in ways the new client may not have heard before. It might seem like having to learn a new language. In this space, please list words you've heard in treatment or therapy that are new to you or are being used in new ways you're not used to hearing.

_____

_____

_____

2.   The new client may also get the impression that he or she will have to learn a whole new set of skills to solve the problems that brought him or her into treatment. When staff and fellow clients talk about what has to be done to stay clean and sober, these terms are often equally unfamiliar. Please list any methods you've heard people talking about that seem foreign and unfamiliar.

_____

_____

_____

3.   The impression discussed in Question 2 is misleading. None of us grow up without learning some ways to solve problems in our lives, and many of those methods will work on any kind of problem, including addiction and substance abuse. Of course, using alcohol or other drugs was one of your problem-solving tools itself, and that one is obviously not going to work here. But you have used many other methods to solve problems

already in your life. In this space, please list five situations where you have solved a problem or accomplished a goal.

a. _____

b. _____

c. _____

d. _____

e. _____

4. Now, please examine this list of problem-solving/goal-accomplishing skills, traits, and methods, and check off the ones you used in the five situations you just listed.

__ Asking others for help

__ Being alert

__ Being decisive

__ Being flexible

__ Being open-minded

__ Being patient

__ Being persistent

__ Brainstorming—generating lots of ideas, then picking out the best ones

__ Breaking a big problem down into small steps

__ Showing courtesy

__ Defining a goal and steps to reach it

__ Determining tools suited for a job

__ Explaining to others

__ Finding alternative ways to do things

__ Following instructions

__ Helping others

__ Listening carefully

__ Negotiating

__ Organizing other people

__ Paying attention to details

___ Planning use of time

___ Practicing an easy task, then working up to harder ones

___ Practicing, period

___ Praying

___ Recognizing patterns

___ Researching needed information (asking people, using books, using the Internet, etc.)

___ Sharing

___ Studying

___ Taking notes

___ Using humor

___ Using a method that worked in a similar situation

___ Using persuasion

___ Using trial and error

___ Watching others, then using the same methods

___ Working alone

___ Working in a team

5. As you can see, the process of solving problems breaks down into skills that can be used in many different situations, and even if you haven't faced this particular problem before, you already have many of the skills that will enable you to succeed. Now go back and circle the skills or strengths you think will help you to gain and maintain sober recovery from abuse of, or dependence on, alcohol or other drugs.

6. The items from this list that most people find most useful in staying clean and sober are: all of the above! However, each individual uses them differently. Please go over the list in Question 4 carefully, and pick the five items that are most important in your problem-solving approach—in other words, which five do you use the most? After you pick your top five, write an example of how you can use each to work on your recovery. For example, if you picked "researching information," some ways you could use this might be reading books on several different approaches to staying clean and sober, talking to people who are succeeding at the same task, finding Web sites on the Internet with information about recovery from addiction, and so on.

Problem-solving skill or trait   *How I can use it in recovery*

a. _____   _____

_____

_____

b. _____   _____

_____

_____

c. _____   _____

_____

_____

d. _____   _____

_____

_____

e. _____   _____

_____

_____

7. Many alcoholics and addicts, once they get the chemicals out of their systems, find that they are smart, creative, funny, hardworking, loyal, and generous. How many of those words fit you? What qualities in you do others value? Talk to three people who know you well. Ask them what qualities and abilities of yours they think will be most helpful to you in staying clean and sober. Write their answers here.

_____

_____

_____

_____

_____

8. Finally, here are ways in which some particular skills and strengths can help people in recovery. If you have these skills or strengths, here are ways you can use them:

    a. *Good communication skills:* Working with others—clinical staff, recovery program members, sponsors, clergy, friends, family

    b. *High energy and determination:* Continuing to work your program even when you're temporarily discouraged; helping others

c. *Sense of humor:* Coping with difficult or painful moments; avoiding self-pity or false pride; enjoying fellowship with other recovering people

d. *Spirituality:* Improving a relationship with a Higher Power; staying clear on what your values are; having faith to carry you through hard times

e. *Creativity:* Finding new ways to help yourself and others; putting old tools to new uses

9. Think about the parts of getting and staying clean and sober that are the hardest or most nerve-wracking for you; pick three specific problems or situations that worry you. Write them in this space, then write a few sentences for each describing how you can use the methods and qualities we've been talking about to tackle each of those three issues. After you've finished this handout, talk about it with your therapist or group the next time you meet.

Problem #1: _____

How I can tackle it: _____

_____

_____

Problem #2: _____

How I can tackle it: _____

_____

_____

Problem #3: _____

How I can tackle it: _____

_____

_____

Above all, remember that whatever questions or problems you face in recovery, others have faced them before you. If they succeeded, so can you—just pick out someone who is a lot like you and overcame similar problems, find out what he or she did, and do the same thing.

Remember to bring completed work sheet to your next appointment.

Who Can Help Me?
Identifying and Building
My Support Network

GOALS OF THE EXERCISE

1. To help the client identify and get help from supportive others at home, at work, and in other settings.
2. To decrease the client's feeling of isolation and hasten reintegration into his or her community.
3. To encourage healthy interdependence rather than either enmeshed codependence or unsupported isolation.

TYPES OF PROBLEMS THIS EXERCISE MAY BE MOST USEFUL FOR

*   Adult Children of Alcoholic (ACOA) Traits
*   Anxiety
*   Borderline Traits
*   Codependency
*   Depression
*   Emotional Isolation
*   Hopelessness
*   Inadequate Support Network
*   Learned Helplessness
*   Living Environment Deficiencies (Relapse Triggers, Lack of Emotional Support, etc.)
*   Low Self-Esteem
*   Poor Social Skills
*   Post-acute Withdrawal
*   Posttraumatic Stress Issues
*   Recent Bereavement/Loss
*   Shame Issues
*   Spiritual Confusion

- Substance Abuse
- Substance Dependence
- Suicidality
- Tendency to Repeated Relapse

SUGGESTIONS FOR PROCESSING THIS EXERCISE WITH CLIENT

1. How have others helped you so far?
2. How have you been able to help others at this point?
3. What do you think about the idea of asking others for help—can you do that? Have you already done it, for example by coming here?
4. What are the ways you see people work on recovery together more effectively than alone?

WHO CAN HELP ME? IDENTIFYING AND BUILDING MY SUPPORT NETWORK

A common tendency of practicing alcoholics and addicts is self-isolation, and reversing that trait is an important part of early recovery. Most people who succeed in achieving long-term abstinence from addictive substances and behavior do so with the help of others, not alone.

1. Often when people first come into a treatment program or therapy for drug or alcohol problems, they have great difficulty asking anyone for anything, and especially for help with a problem. Does this describe you? _____ What makes this difficult for you?

   _____

   _____

   _____

2. If the situation is reversed, and you find yourself associating with someone who is brand-new in an area where you have some knowledge and experience, how does it make you feel if that person turns to you and asks for your help or advice?

   _____

   _____

3. Do you see others in treatment or early recovery getting help and support from people who have been in recovery longer? Does it change the way you think of these people to see them acknowledge that they don't know something and ask someone who does know? What do you think of this when you see someone else do it?

   _____

   _____

4. What kinds of responses do you usually see these people get from those they ask for help or guidance? Are these responses you would like to get, or give, in a similar situation?

   _____

   _____

61

5. What are some specific areas in which you could use some information, some support, and some feedback on how you're doing? Please list three such areas—pick things that confuse you or seem extra difficult.

    _____

    _____

    _____

6. Now think about who is apparently successful in those areas. List some people by name, and then circle the categories of people you think would be helpful to you.

Names	Categories
_____	Family members
_____	Friends
_____	Coworkers
_____	Support group members
_____	Mental health professionals
_____	Clergymen and women
_____	Medical professionals
_____	Educators

7. Now think about how you might ask each of these people for some assistance and support in your efforts at recovery. You will probably want to communicate these things:

a. What you are trying to accomplish—to stay clean and sober and change your way of life

b. What specific goal you have set as your way to measure your success for now. This can be something like staying sober for a year, working the Twelve Steps, finding six new activities to replace drinking and using, and so on

c. What specific problems you are having difficulty with at this moment

d. How you feel these people can help you achieve your goals and solve your problems (be careful not to make it sound as if you think they'll do it for you, unless it's a special problem and that's their job!)

e. Why you chose them over others to ask for assistance

8. When you have identified people who will help you work on your recovery, the next step is to establish a routine with each of them. Most of us are busy enough that we fail to get

around to things unless they are scheduled. This can vary with the people involved and the situation. For example, you might meet with a therapist at a set time each week; have dinner with family on certain nights; call a friend at about the same time each weekend; go to a particular support group meeting daily or weekly; or have lunch with a sponsor regularly. For each of the people you named, when will you meet or talk with them?

Name	When/where/how I will meet or talk with this person

9. It can also be an important part of your recovery work to help others in whatever way you can. For example, you might volunteer a few hours a week to do some sort of service work as a volunteer; if you belong to a Twelve-Step group, you can volunteer for service chores such as making coffee, setting up furniture, cleaning up after meetings, and so on. What kind of service to others will you include in your recovery program, and when and where will you do it?

Service task	For whom	Time	Place

Remember to bring completed work sheet to your next appointment.

What Works for Other People?
Learning from Recovery Role Models

GOALS OF THE EXERCISE

1. To help the client learn vicariously from others who are succeeding in solving the same problems.
2. To set the stage for the client to bond to a community of like-minded people pursuing the same goals.
3. To encourage healthy interdependence rather than either enmeshed codependence or unsupported isolation.

TYPES OF PROBLEMS THIS EXERCISE MAY BE MOST USEFUL FOR

- Anger Management
- Anxiety
- Borderline Traits
- Burnout
- Codependency
- Depression
- Emotional Isolation
- General Interpersonal Relational Problems
- Grandiosity
- Hopelessness
- Inadequate Support Network
- Learned Helplessness
- Living Environment Deficiencies (Relapse Triggers, Lack of Emotional Support, etc.)
- Low Self-Esteem
- Occupational Problems
- Parent-Child Relational Problems
- Partner Relational Problems

- Peer Group Negativity
- Poor Social Skills
- Post-acute Withdrawal
- Posttraumatic Stress Issues
- Recent Bereavement/Loss
- Shame Issues
- Spiritual Confusion
- Substance Abuse
- Substance Dependence
- Tendency to Repeated Relapse

SUGGESTIONS FOR PROCESSING THIS EXERCISE WITH CLIENT

1. Do you feel as if you fit in with the people you're in contact with in treatment or at support group meetings? What is the common bond you sense with them—how are you alike?
2. Do you see others who are like you succeeding at the goals you are working on? Does that change your feelings about your own chances of success?
3. If the situation were reversed, how do you think you'd feel to know someone was using you as an example or role model to pattern his or her actions after?

WHAT WORKS FOR OTHER PEOPLE?
LEARNING FROM RECOVERY ROLE MODELS

> *One of the most striking common experiences most alcoholics and addicts report having when they get involved in recovery work, either through therapy or a support group, is that for the first time they feel that they fit in. They have found people who are like them. Given this situation, it seems a commonsense idea that what works for these others who are like the newly recovering person might work for him or her as well. Usually this is the case. In this exercise you will examine the successes of other people who are enough like you that their methods should work for you as well.*

1. Since starting treatment, have you met people who have a lot in common with you and who are succeeding at getting clean and sober and staying that way? If this is something you have tried without success before, does seeing others who are succeeding change your views about your own chances? _____ How has your outlook on your recovery changed since you started treatment?

    _____

    _____

2. When you talk with people like you who are succeeding at staying away from alcohol and other drugs, what do they tell you are the most important things they are doing to succeed?

    _____

    _____

    _____

3. Here are some of the things people have done to stay clean and sober—check the ones you see others using or hear from them that they use.

    __ Avoiding bars and other places they drank/used

    __ Talking to supportive people when stressed

    __ Going to support group meetings (A.A., etc.)

    __ Working with a Twelve-Step sponsor

    __ Being a Twelve-Step sponsor for others

    __ Avoiding people they drank/used with

    __ Going to therapy

    __ Getting regular exercise

    __ Reading recovery/spiritual material

    __ Keeping a journal

__ Socializing with sober friends

__ Laughing at least once a day

__ Making a recovery/relapse prevention plan

__ Going to church

__ Helping others stay clean and sober

__ Praying daily

__ HALT: Not getting too hungry, angry, lonely, or tired

4. During the next week, your assignment is to talk with a different recovering person each day and ask each person what actions help him or her stay clean and sober. Write the answers here.

Day 1: _____

Day 2: _____

Day 3: _____

Day 4: _____

Day 5: _____

Day 6: _____

Day 7: _____

5. Now you are in a position to pick and choose the methods that seem best suited to your personality and your situation. Ideally you should have four types of strategies to stay sober. You will want strategies that you can use alone and strategies that allow you and others to help one another; you will also want strategies for very specific situations and strategies that are useful for nearly all situations. Please fill in this matrix now with at least two methods per square.

	Methods for one person	Methods for a team
Methods for specific situations		
Methods for general use in any situation		

6. Lastly, it can be useful to notice what has *not* worked for others, especially others like you. Your assignment is to talk to at least five recovering people, or to bring this topic up in a therapy or support group meeting, and ask people what they have seen others try or tried themselves to avoid relapse, but without succeeding. List some actions that didn't work.

    _____   _____   _____

    _____   _____   _____

    _____   _____   _____

Remember to bring completed work sheet to your next appointment.

Identifying and Using Community Resources

GOALS OF THE EXERCISE

1. To help the client make effective use of available resources to assist in personal and family recovery from substance dependence and abuse and related problems.
2. To reduce emotional and social isolation for clients and their family members.
3. To increase the effectiveness of treatment and aftercare by augmenting them with resources that clients can use indefinitely without cost restraints.

TYPES OF PROBLEMS THIS EXERCISE MAY BE MOST USEFUL FOR

- Adult Children of Alcoholic (ACOA) Traits
- Anxiety
- Codependency
- Depression
- Emotional Isolation
- Hopelessness
- Inadequate Support Network
- Legal Problems
- Learned Helplessness
- Living Environment Deficiencies (Relapse Triggers, Lack of Emotional Support, etc.)
- Low Self-Esteem
- Medical Issues
- Mood Swings
- Occupational Problems
- Parent-Child Relational Problems
- Partner Relational Problems
- Poor Social Skills
- Post-acute Withdrawal

- Posttraumatic Stress Issues
- Recent Bereavement/Loss
- Resistance Based on Distorted Beliefs about Support Groups
- Shame Issues
- Spiritual Confusion
- Substance Abuse
- Substance Dependence
- Suicidality
- Tendency to Repeated Relapse
- Treatment/Aftercare Noncompliance
- Unresolved Childhood Trauma
- Unresolved Grief and Loss
- Value Conflicts

SUGGESTIONS FOR PROCESSING THIS EXERCISE WITH CLIENT

1. Of the community resources mentioned in this exercise, which one is the first you'll be contacting?
2. How many of these community resources did you know about before this exercise? Do you know other people who could benefit by getting this information?
3. How do you think you might be able to help others you meet through your use of these groups, information sources, and other resources?

IDENTIFYING AND USING
COMMUNITY RESOURCES

A common trait of alcoholics, addicts, and people who grew up with abuse, neglect, or other hardships or deprivations is a tendency to be so self-sufficient they don't think of turning to others for help or information. Even when you are in treatment, it may not occur to you that you can also get help with other issues, and that it may be wise to do so. This exercise is meant to focus your attention on the sources of emotional and practical support and help that are available for your use and the use of your family.

1. *Treatment programs:* There are several kinds of community resources you might find useful. The first type is the treatment program. Depending on the kind of treatment you are receiving, you may be in a treatment program now. However, there are treatment programs for many other problems beyond drug and alcohol issues, and you or someone in your family might benefit from another kind of treatment program. What types of problems can you think of that might be helped by treatment programs in your community?

    _____

    _____

    Here are some other types of treatment programs—check the ones you feel might be helpful for yourself or someone close to you.

    Although they vary in many ways, treatment programs usually have these things in common:

    *   They charge for their services (often your health insurance will pay), although some are able to offer free services in return for participating in research studies, or because they are paid for by government agencies, universities, or businesses.
    *   They are run by professionals (doctors, psychologists, therapists, social workers, etc.) who are in charge and decide what people need to do to solve their problems.
    *   They may be residential (meaning clients or patients live there while in treatment) or outpatient, but they are usually intensive and take a lot of time while you are in treatment.
    *   Treatment through these programs usually lasts for several days or weeks, then ends.
    *   They have their own facilities where they provide their services.
    *   Clients or patients usually don't have much to do with each other away from the treatment program, and there may even be rules against socializing outside of treatment.

71

__ Eating disorders (anorexia, bulimia, compulsive overeating)

__ Compulsive gambling

__ Depression, anxiety, and other emotional or mental disturbances

__ Codependency and other relationship problems

__ Violence and antisocial behavior in children

__ Physical, sexual, or emotional abuse and trauma

__ Smoking

How do you feel about the idea that each of these problems affects many people seriously enough to lead to the creation of organized treatment programs to overcome them? If you or someone close to you suffers from one of these problems, how does this change the way you think about solving that problem?

_____

_____

2. *Support groups:* Another community resource, possibly the first one most people would think of, is the support group. Support groups exist for nearly every problem people have, especially in large communities. Alcoholics Anonymous (A.A.) and Narcotics Anonymous (N.A.) are two examples, but there are many others. Many are Twelve-Step programs like A.A. and N.A., but there are also quite a few other types of support groups. The things support groups usually have in common are:

- They are normally free, or collect only small fees.
- Rather than being run by professionals, they are run in a more democratic way by their members, who treat each other as equals and take a teamwork approach to solving problems and achieving goals.
- They meet at set times in public places, such as schools, churches, synagogues, temples, restaurants, or meeting rooms at businesses.
- Members often socialize together away from the support group meetings.
- Your participation can usually last as long as you want it to, rather than being on a set schedule like a treatment program. Some members attend for the rest of their lives.

Here is a partial list of problems or situations that have led to support groups forming to help people deal with them—your community probably has some or all of these groups. Again, please check any that would be useful to you or someone you know, or might have been useful for you in the past.

__ Sufferers of addictive or compulsive problems including alcoholism, addiction, eating, gambling, spending on credit, workaholism, destructive relationships, sex addiction, Internet addiction, and smoking

__ Family members of alcoholics, addicts, or gamblers

__ Sufferers of emotional and mental illness and their families and friends

__ Divorced people

__ Family and friends of Alzheimer's disease sufferers

__ Parents who are afraid they will get so angry they will hurt their children

__ Parents whose children have died

__ Widows and widowers

__ Families and friends of suicides

__ Survivors of abuse, assault, rape, and other violent crimes

__ Sufferers of various specific illnesses or injuries and their families and friends

Unless you are very unusual, one or more of these issues has affected your life. How would it be different for you to have the advice and support of a whole group of people who understood what you were going through because they had experienced the same things? How would that be different from trying to cope with a problem alone?

_____

_____

_____

3. *Family assistance programs:* In addition to treatment programs and support groups, there are many kinds of family assistance programs out there. They are run by organizations including government agencies, churches, synagogues, temples, social clubs, schools and universities, and private companies. The assistance they provide may take several forms. Please check off whichever types of assistance you feel you or your family could use.

__ Transportation for work, shopping, medical treatment, therapy, school, or other purposes

__ Sports and hobby training and activities

__ Help with free or low-cost food

__ Clothing

__ Housing assistance

__ Parenting skills training

__ Coping with disabilities

__ Help for single parents in raising their children (usually by having an adult spend time with the child, giving him or her a good role model and giving the parent a break from being the only person in charge of the child)

Again, if one of these is a problem you have been struggling with alone or with only the help of family or friends, what do you think of the idea of an organized group being available to you to back you up?

_____

_____

4. *Educational and vocational programs:* These programs help people learn to read and write, learn English, complete their high school diplomas or GEDs, and learn job skills, among other things. They are normally run by colleges or public school systems. Are there things you would like to go back to school to learn? If so, what are they?

_____

_____

If you live in a large town or a city, there's a good chance someone offers a program that will teach you what you need to learn. Some of these programs are free, some are inexpensive, and some are costly. You can usually find high school completion and GED programs that are free or cost very little, while some trade schools teaching specific job skills like plumbing, welding, auto mechanics, and so on may be fairly expensive.

5. *Religious and spiritual programs:* Depending on your views, this is an area that might be important to you or one you have little interest in. Some people, even people who start recovery with no interest in spirituality, do find that spiritual help is very important in their lives. A.A. and the other Twelve-Step programs all have a strong spiritual focus, although they are not churches and do not tell members how to manage their spiritual lives. The other place to find these programs, obviously, is in connection with churches, synagogues, and temples. The programs are normally free of charge and while they may not solve practical problems like paying the rent, they can help people figure out what goals they want to achieve and what is really important in their lives. Are you interested in religious or spiritual programs? _____ If so, what do you want to change about your life that a religious or spiritual program might help you with?

_____

_____

6. *Sources of information:* Almost every community has at least one library. This and other sources of information can help you in many ways. Libraries not only have books with information on almost anything you want to accomplish in your life, in most cases they also have computers with Internet access. These are usually available for you to use free of charge. Other sources of information include knowledgeable people (doctors, teachers, counselors and therapists, etc.), education programs on TV, and the newspaper. Many communities have free newspaper-type publications with useful information in every issue. What sources of information are available to you personally right now?

_____

_____

_____

7. Now that we've looked at a wide range of community resources that might be able to back you in your efforts to overcome problems and achieve your goals, how do you find these resources? They can be located in several ways (again, check off all that are available to you):

___ Your therapist can give you information about resources in your community.

___ You can look resources up in the telephone directory.

___ Resources often advertise in the newspapers.

___ TV news and educational TV programs may give you this information.

___ Bulletin boards in the community often have information you can use (you can find these bulletin boards at schools, colleges, government agencies, laundromats, restaurants, medical offices, churches, synagogues, temples, and many other places).

___ You can call information lines, usually listed in the telephone directory.

Now your task is to think about what kinds of help you and your family could use, talk to your therapist, and make a plan for how you will look for community resources to give you information or support you need. Please use this space to write about types of assistance you want, where you will go to find that assistance, and when you plan to do this.

_____

_____

_____

_____

_____

_____

Remember to bring completed work sheet to your next appointment.

Using Books, Videos, Audiotapes, and Other Media Resources

GOALS OF THE EXERCISE

1. To help the client find and make effective use of media resources to assist in personal and family recovery from substance dependence and abuse and related problems.
2. To reduce shame and emotional isolation by helping the client see that his or her issues also affect so many other people that they are the subjects of mass media attention.
3. To increase the effectiveness of treatment and aftercare by augmenting them with resources that clients can use outside of the treatment environment.

TYPES OF PROBLEMS THIS EXERCISE MAY BE MOST USEFUL FOR

- Adult Children of Alcoholic (ACOA) Traits
- Anger Management
- Anxiety
- Appetite Disturbance
- Blaming/Projection/Failure to Take Appropriate Responsibility
- Borderline Traits
- Burnout
- Codependency
- Denial/Rationalization/Minimization of Substance-Abusing Behavior and/or Relapse Risk
- Depression
- Emotional Isolation
- Family Conflict
- General Interpersonal Relational Problems
- Generalized Treatment Resistance
- History of Self-Medication for Mood/Pain Problems
- Hopelessness
- Issues of Identity

- Legal Problems
- Learned Helplessness
- Living Environment Deficiencies (Relapse Triggers, Lack of Emotional Support, etc.)
- Low Self-Esteem
- Medical Issues
- Mood Swings
- Occupational Problems
- Parent-Child Relational Problems
- Partner Relational Problems
- Peer Group Negativity
- Poor Social Skills
- Posttraumatic Stress Issues
- Recent Bereavement/Loss
- Resistance Based on Distorted Beliefs about Substance Abuse/Dependence
- Resistance Based on Distorted Beliefs about Support Groups
- Shame Issues
- Spiritual Confusion
- Substance Abuse
- Substance Dependence
- Suicidality
- Tendency to Repeated Relapse
- Treatment/Aftercare Noncompliance
- Unresolved Childhood Trauma
- Unresolved Grief and Loss
- Value Conflicts

SUGGESTIONS FOR PROCESSING THIS EXERCISE WITH CLIENT

1. What type of media resources do you like to use?
2. Have you seen good films or TV shows or read good books about problems that affect your life before now?
3. Think back over your life up to now. Of all the films, TV shows, songs, or books you've experienced, which ones had strong emotional effects on you, and why do you think they affected you so much?
4. It is suggested that the therapist obtain a copy of the excellent book entitled *Rent Two Films and Let's Talk in the Morning* (Hesley and Hesley, 1998). This book discusses ways to integrate video-viewing "homework" into therapy using widely available commercially produced films. The Hesleys provide extensive recommendations for using specific films to address various treatment issues.

USING BOOKS, VIDEOS, AUDIOTAPES, AND OTHER MEDIA RESOURCES

Because they affect so many people that they are important parts of every culture, the issues you are working on in treatment have inspired people to create many films, TV shows, books, and pieces of art and music about those issues. Often these films, books, and other materials can give us useful information or inspiration, or they can move us emotionally in a powerful way that can help treatment. This exercise aims to get you thinking about how you can use some of this material to help you achieve your own goals.

1. Have you seen films or TV shows, read books, or listened to music that dealt with issues of substance abuse or other problems that may go together with drinking or drug use? What was the piece of work you were exposed to, and what feelings did it cause in you?

    _____

    _____

2. How do you feel these works could help you or others overcome the problems that brought you into treatment?

    _____

    _____

3. Here are some places you can get these materials. Please check all that are available to you wherever you live.

    Free sources   *Sources that cost money*

    __ Libraries   __ Bookstores

    __ The Internet   __ Video rental/sales outlets

    __ Community agencies   __ Movie theaters

4. Talk with your therapist, and choose the first video, TV program, book, or piece of music you will use as part of your therapy. Please watch, read, or listen to this work, then write here about whatever feelings or thoughts you had as a reaction.

    _____

    _____

    _____

Remember to bring completed work sheet to your next appointment.

Section IV

Planning Strategies and Taking Action

Meeting My Needs:
Alternatives to Substance Use

GOALS OF THE EXERCISE

1. To encourage the client to participate in activities that are pleasurable as constructive and healthy alternatives to the use of alcohol or other drugs.
2. To offer the idea that the client got some needs met by using substances, but also suffered unacceptable negative consequences, and that that life without chemicals must include finding ways to meet those needs that do not involve substance abuse.

TYPES OF PROBLEMS THIS EXERCISE MAY BE MOST USEFUL FOR

- Antisocial Behavior
- Denial/Rationalization/Minimization of Substance-Abusing Behavior and/or Relapse Risk
- Depression
- Emotional Isolation
- Generalized Treatment Resistance
- History of Self-Medication for Mood/Pain Problems
- Impulsivity
- Learned Helplessness
- Living Environment Deficiencies (Relapse Triggers, Lack of Emotional Support, etc.)
- Low Self-Esteem
- Medical Issues
- Occupational Problems
- Parent-Child Relational Problems
- Partner Relational Problems
- Peer Group Negativity
- Poor Social Skills
- Recent Bereavement/Loss

- Resistance Based on Distorted Beliefs about Substance Abuse/Dependence
- Shame Issues
- Sleep Disturbance
- Spiritual Confusion
- Substance Abuse
- Substance Dependence
- Substance Withdrawal
- Suicidality
- Tendency to Repeated Relapse
- Treatment/Aftercare Noncompliance
- Unresolved Grief and Loss
- Value Conflicts

SUGGESTIONS FOR PROCESSING THIS EXERCISE WITH CLIENT

1. What needs did substances meet for you, and what alternative activities will you use to replace drinking or drug use in meetings those needs?
2. What problems must you overcome first to engage in any of these alternative activities?

MEETING MY NEEDS: ALTERNATIVES TO SUBSTANCE USE

For many recovering people, most of the things they did for fun or relaxation involved drinking or using other drugs, with destructive consequences. Thinking about what you like to do and ways to get your needs met that do not involve substance abuse is largely a matter of reeducation. This exercise will assist you in identifying more positive and non-substance-using alternatives to get your personal needs met and find enjoyment.

1. List all the benefits you can think of that you got from drinking or other drug use.

    Physical   *Social*   *Mental or emotional*

    _____   _____   _____

    _____   _____   _____

    _____   _____   _____

    _____   _____   _____

    _____   _____   _____

2. Now list as many drawbacks as you can think of connected with drinking or other drug use.

    Physical   *Social*   *Mental or emotional*

    _____   _____   _____

    _____   _____   _____

    _____   _____   _____

    _____   _____   _____

    _____   _____   _____

3. List the benefits you can think of connected with abstinence from alcohol or other drugs.

Physical	*Social*	*Mental or emotional*
_____	_____	_____
_____	_____	_____
_____	_____	_____
_____	_____	_____
_____	_____	_____

4. List the drawbacks you see connected with abstinence from drinking or other drug use.

Physical	*Social*	*Mental or emotional*
_____	_____	_____
_____	_____	_____
_____	_____	_____
_____	_____	_____
_____	_____	_____

5. Brainstorm activity: List as many alternative ways as you can think of to get the benefits you listed for drinking or other drug use without the same or equal negative consequences.

Physical	*Social*	*Mental or emotional*
_____	_____	_____
_____	_____	_____
_____	_____	_____
_____	_____	_____
_____	_____	_____

6. List three activities that:

a. You enjoy: _____

_____

b. You would enjoy, but haven't tried:_____

_____

85

c. You've heard others talk about and are interested in: _____

_____

d. You could enjoy doing alone: _____

_____

e. You could enjoy doing with others:_____

_____

7. I am making a commitment to myself to take the following step within the next week to start practicing an alternative activity:

_____

_____

Remember to bring completed work sheet to your next appointment.

Using My Support Network

GOALS OF THE EXERCISE

1. To encourage the client to work with others versus trying to get well alone.
2. To identify the ways a support network can assist the client in his or her efforts at recovery.

TYPES OF PROBLEMS THIS EXERCISE MAY BE MOST USEFUL FOR

- Adult Children of Alcoholic (ACOA) Traits
- Anger Management
- Anxiety
- Borderline Traits
- Codependency
- Depression
- Emotional Isolation
- Hopelessness
- Inadequate Support Network
- Learned Helplessness
- Living Environment Deficiencies (Relapse Triggers, Lack of Emotional Support, etc.)
- Low Self-Esteem
- Parent-child Relational Problems
- Partner Relational Problems
- Peer Group Negativity
- Poor Social Skills
- Post-acute Withdrawal
- Resistance Based on Distorted Beliefs about Support Groups
- Shame Issues
- Spiritual Confusion

- Substance Abuse
- Substance Dependence
- Substance Withdrawal
- Suicidality
- Tendency to Repeated Relapse
- Unresolved Childhood Trauma
- Unresolved Grief and Loss

SUGGESTIONS FOR PROCESSING THIS EXERCISE WITH CLIENT

1. What information do you need to share with people in your support network in order for them to help you?
2. Role-play: Rehearse how you will ask someone for assistance in staying clean and sober.
3. If someone else asked you to help him or her prevent a relapse, how could you help? Would you like someone to help you in the same way?

USING MY SUPPORT NETWORK

It is common for people dealing with substance abuse/dependence to isolate themselves or feel embarrassed or ashamed about their histories. Also, some feel that since they got themselves into the messes they are in, they need to solve their own problems. However, people who are embarking on this journey and learning new skills benefit when they seek help from others who care about them, or who are succeeding in achieving the same goals or implementing the new skills. This exercise is designed to get you started using the support of those people you have identified as helpful to increase your success in making these lifestyle changes.

1. The supportive people I will ask to help me stay clean and sober are:

   Family: _____

   Friends: _____

   Work/school: _____

   Spiritual/religious:_____

   Community: _____

   Other: _____

2. The benefits I will get from working with my support network are:

   _____

3. The biggest obstacle or barrier for me in asking for assistance is:

   _____

4. The best thing that could happen when I ask someone for help is:

   _____

5. The worst thing that could happen when I ask someone for help is:

   _____

6. Write what you will tell your supports about how you would like them to help you.

_____

_____

_____

_____

_____

_____

_____

_____

_____

_____

Remember to bring completed work sheet to your next appointment.

Stress Management

GOALS OF THE EXERCISE

1. To identify sources and common reactions to stress and give the client a gauge for measuring future changes in his or her reactions to stress.
2. To help the client identify effective stress management methods he or she is already using.
3. To encourage the client to incorporate stress management as part of a lifestyle change and identify areas in which to begin modifying his or her stress responses.

TYPES OF PROBLEMS THIS EXERCISE MAY BE MOST USEFUL FOR

- Adult Children of Alcoholic (ACOA) Traits
- Anger Management
- Antisocial Behavior
- Anxiety
- Borderline Traits
- Burnout
- Codependency
- Depression
- Emotional Isolation
- Family Conflict
- General Interpersonal Relational Problems
- History of Self-Medication for Mood/Pain Problems
- Inadequate Support Network
- Legal Problems
- Low Self-Esteem
- Medical Issues
- Occupational Problems

- Post-acute Withdrawal
- Posttraumatic Stress Issues
- Recent Bereavement/Loss
- Sleep Disturbance
- Substance Abuse
- Substance Dependence
- Substance Withdrawal
- Suicidality
- Tendency to Repeated Relapse

SUGGESTIONS FOR PROCESSING THIS EXERCISE WITH CLIENT

1. What was the imagination exercise like for you—what did you experience?
2. What new insights do you have into your stress management style?
3. How will you use the information in this workbook in your recovery?

STRESS MANAGEMENT

At least one-third of relapses are triggered by stressful situations, probably because many chemically dependent and substance-abusing people have used alcohol or other drugs as a tool for handling stress. You have choices: Find a way to guarantee you will never again experience stress, or find a different way to handle it. The purpose of this exercise is to teach you about your own stress management style, your sources of stress, and how you can manage stress differently and more effectively.

1. Please describe a situation in which you used alcohol/other drugs to cope with stress.

   _____

   _____

2. What connections do you see between stress and alcohol or other drugs in your life?

   _____

   _____

3. What kinds of situations cause you stress? Please list three situations that commonly trigger stress for you.

   _____

   _____

   _____

4. How can you tell when you are experiencing stress in your life? Please list your reactions to stress, both physical and emotional.

   _____

   _____

   _____

5. What are your usual ways of handling stress?

   _____

   _____

6. Please talk with some people who know you well and whom you feel have good judgment, people you trust to give you straight answers. Ask them to describe in a phrase or short sentence what they have seen as your usual reactions to stress. Write their answers here.

    _____

    _____

7. List causes of stress you can control.   List actions you can take to cope.

    _____   _____

    _____   _____

    _____   _____

    _____   _____

8. List causes of stress beyond your control.   List thoughts about these you can change.

    _____   _____

    _____   _____

    _____   _____

9. Describe a stressful situation you handled well and how you did it.

    _____

    _____

    _____

10. You can reduce your level of stress by not overdoing things in any area of your life. This can reduce the stress you experience and help you do better handling what stress remains. Please list at least one thing you can do today to create more balance in each area listed here.

    a. Relationships with family or friends: _____

    _____

    b. Leisure time/activities: _____

    _____

    c. Work/school: _____

    _____

d. Community involvement: _____

_____

e. Spiritual activities: _____

_____

f. Diet: _____

_____

g. Exercise: _____

_____

h. Emotions: _____

_____

11. What will you do differently when confronted with stressful situations in your recovery?

_____

_____

_____

12. Imagination exercise: Picture yourself in the future, handling a stressful situation employing different and more effective methods than you would have when you were drinking or using. What improvements do you see in the results and your quality of life over the way things are now? What are you already doing differently, and what can you start doing now, to change your present situation to the one you imagined? While you picture yourself living this way, pay attention to how that image of yourself makes you feel. Talk about this with other members of the treatment group or in your next treatment session.

_____

_____

_____

_____

_____

_____

_____

_____

_____

Remember to bring completed work sheet to your next appointment.

Communication Skills

GOALS OF THE EXERCISE

1. To assist the client in identifying ways he or she currently succeeds and fails in sharing thoughts, feelings, or problems with others.
2. To help the client identify better ways to communicate and learn to use them.
3. To equip the client to teach more effective communication strategies to others in his or her life and use these strategies in those relationships.

TYPES OF PROBLEMS THIS EXERCISE MAY BE MOST USEFUL FOR

*   Adult Children of Alcoholic (ACOA) Traits
*   Anger Management
*   Antisocial Behavior
*   Borderline Traits
*   Codependency
*   Emotional Isolation
*   General Interpersonal Relational Problems
*   Occupational Problems
*   Parent-Child Relational Problems
*   Partner Relational Problems
*   Poor Social Skills

SUGGESTIONS FOR PROCESSING THIS EXERCISE WITH CLIENT

1. What did you learn about your communication style?
2. What difficulties did you experience in practicing the steps to effective communication?
3. What successes did you experience in practicing the skills?
4. Practice the skills in session, role-playing situations and people that the client has particular difficulty with.

COMMUNICATION SKILLS

Saying what you mean in a way that is respectful both to yourself and to others is a skill that can be learned, and so is hearing what others are trying to share with you. Effective communication requires two basic skills: expressing yourself clearly, and listening actively. In completing this exercise you will learn styles of communication and steps to more effective communication.

1. To start, please list the people with whom you have the most trouble communicating, and why you believe this happens; then do the same for people with whom you find it easy to communicate.

    People with whom I have difficulty communicating   *Reasons*

    _____   _____

    _____   _____

    _____   _____

    _____   _____

    _____   _____

    People with whom I find it easy to communicate   *Reasons*

    _____   _____

    _____   _____

    _____   _____

    _____   _____

    _____   _____

2. Now we will examine some communication styles and how they work. Although we all use different communication styles in different situations, we each have a favored style we use the most. While you read about the following styles, think about your own habits and those of other people in your life.

a. *Aggressive:* Expressing yourself with an attitude of intimidation; little regard for others' rights, thoughts, or feelings. Aggressive communication can be abusive, threatening, and judgmental, and may include name-calling, yelling, interrupting, sarcasm, ridicule, and hostile body language

b. *Passive-aggressive:* Not expressing yourself openly, but instead hinting, being indirect, or being silent about what you want, think, or feel; talking behind others' backs; being sarcastic; pouting; whining; constant complaining; expecting others to know what you think, feel, or want without your telling them; refusing to talk even though visibly upset

c. *Passive:* Not feeling you have a right to feelings or opinions or the right to express yourself in any way that might upset others, or possibly any way at all; giving short, uninformative answers; agreeing with whatever others say

d. *Assertive:* Expressing your thoughts, feelings, and wishes without ignoring those of others; being able to disagree openly and say no in a way that respects both others and yourself.

Which of the styles just listed best describes your style of communication? Please choose one and give some examples of how you use this style.

_____

_____

_____

3. In your relationships with family members, friends, and coworkers, what happens when you disagree with someone or someone disagrees with you?

_____

_____

_____

4. When was the last time you disagreed with someone close to you? How did you handle the situation, and how did the other person react? What was the result?

_____

_____

_____

_____

5. Now we will look at the specific actions that make up effective communication and how you can use them.

a. *Avoid mind-reading:* This means describing what you believe the other person thinks and feels or what you think his or her reasons are for things he or she did. You might be right, but you might be misunderstanding or there might be factors you don't know about. At any rate, most of us get angry or frustrated when others try to tell us what we think or feel, and this often triggers arguments or angry outbursts. *Usually when we mind-read we are not really trying to communicate, we are trying to dominate and control the other person, and no one wants to be dominated or controlled.* Think about the last time someone read your mind in a conversation with you. Describe that situation, how you felt, and whether you feel it helped the communication between you and the other person.

_____

_____

_____

b. *No name-calling:* Usually when we are upset with people it is because of something they did or didn't do: in other words, their actions. Calling people names is not refer-ring to their actions, it is labeling who and what they are. This is frustrating for them, because they may be able to change their actions, but they can't change who and what they are, and when we call them names, we're telling them that this thing they can't change—who and what they are—is wrong or unacceptable. Besides this, name-calling is one of the most proven ways known to trigger anger in someone else and turn a discussion into an argument or a fight. *Usually when we call people names, we are not trying to communicate, we are expressing anger and aggression, and the nat-ural reaction on their part is to become defensive and counterattack.* Think about the last time someone called you a name. Describe that situation, how you felt, and whether you feel it helped the communication between you and the other person.

_____

_____

_____

c. *No interrupting/no long speeches:* These two guidelines go together. When we cut others off (including finishing their sentences for them), the message we are giving them is, "What you have to say is not important enough for any more of my time. Shut up! What I have to say is more important than your thoughts or feelings." Of course, for us to be willing to let the other person talk uninterrupted, we have to know that we will have a chance to express ourselves too. So if we want others to stop interrupting us, we have to give them their time to talk also, and if we monopolize the conversa-tion with long-winded speeches we are denying them that time. *Both interrupting and making long speeches are often ways to control others rather than ways to communi-*

cate effectively, and again, none of us like to be controlled by others. Think about the last time someone went on and on in a conversation with you, or kept interrupting you. Describe that situation, how you felt, and whether you feel it helped the communication between you and the other person.

_____

_____

_____

d. *Be specific:* Again, we usually want someone to change an action, and our chances of getting what we want are better the more we focus on their actions instead of on who and what they are. When we generalize, making statements such as "You always do _____" or "You never do _____," we are really labeling the person more than we are describing a specific action. We are also usually wrong, because even if people *very often* or *very seldom* do something, it is unlikely that they *always* or *never* do it—very few human beings are able to be that consistent. They will probably be able to think of exceptions right away, and they will probably feel hurt that we don't give them credit for those exceptions, and will throw the exceptions back at us to prove we are wrong. This leads to an argument, not to a change in actions that helps us get along better. If we talk about a specific time, place, and event, it is easier to get agreement and change rather than an argument. *If we are generalizing, we are often labeling people rather than their actions, and are much more likely to trigger their defenses than to get them to make a change we want.* Think about the last time someone generalized about your behavior in a conversation with you. Describe that situation, how you felt, and whether you feel it helped the communication between you and the other person.

_____

_____

_____

e. *Stick close to the present:* We may still be feeling angry and hurt over things that happened a long time ago, but if we bring them up in a discussion of something we want to change now, it is more likely to make others feel the situation is hopeless than to achieve the change we want, because people can't change what they did a long time ago. They may be able to admit it and apologize for it, but that works best if it happens in a separate discussion. Especially if people really are trying to change, it causes them frustration if we keep criticizing them for things they did before. To keep tempers under control and avoid turning a discussion into an argument, avoid continually bringing up ancient history. *When we keep dragging up old grievances, it means we haven't finished dealing with them yet, but this is out of place in a talk about the*

101

present and future—it works better to get the present and future taken care of first, then go back and deal with the old problems later. Think about the last time someone brought up old issues in a conversation with you. Describe that situation, how you felt, and whether you feel it helped the communication between you and the other person.

_____

_____

_____

f. *Talk about one thing at a time:* We may have many problems we need to work out with another person, but if we try to work all of them out at once, the other person is likely to feel overwhelmed. Most of us really want to get along with others, and we want them to let us know what they want us to do. But if we feel they want more from us than we can do, we tend to feel angry and frustrated rather than encouraged. When we start bringing up one thing after another in a discussion and throwing them at the other person, it is usually because we are angry and want to vent our frustration. This is sometimes called "kitchen-sink fighting" because it seems to others that we are throwing everything including the kitchen sink at them. *If we really want to solve a particular problem with another person, we are most likely to succeed by keeping our focus on that problem; we may also need to vent our frustrations over other things, but it works better if we don't do it at the same time we are trying to negotiate to solve a problem.* Think about the last time someone threw the kitchen sink at you in a conversation by bringing up unrelated issues. Describe that situation, how you felt, and whether you feel it helped the communication between you and the other person.

_____

_____

_____

g. *Claim your own feelings and actions:* A near-guaranteed way to pick a fight is to tell others that they are responsible for our own feelings or actions by saying "You made me feel _____" or "You made me do _____." Other people can't make us do anything, unless they use physical force to control us. We choose our actions in response to our feelings, thoughts, and wishes. Others can't even make us feel or think a certain way, although they can make it hard for us not to feel or think that way. Our feelings are our own. This is good! Otherwise, we could never be happy if anyone wanted to make us unhappy. Turn it around: Do you want to be held responsible for someone else's actions and feelings? *Do you feel you have enough control over any other person to accept responsibility for what that person does and feels, or is that person likely to feel or act in a way you didn't intend and don't want to feel responsible for? We don't have that much power over others, and they don't have it over us. To avoid this way of starting a fight, it works better to say something like "When you did _____, I felt _____."* Think about the last time someone blamed you for his or her feelings or actions. Describe that situation, how you felt, and whether you feel it helped the communication between you and the other person.

_____

_____

_____

h. *Get and give frequent feedback:* It is easy for people to misunderstand one another. To make sure we are communicating clearly, it is very useful to check with the other person to make sure they understood what we meant. When the other person is talking, it is equally useful to make sure we understand them. The best way to do this is for the listener to repeat the speaker's message back, putting it in his or her own words rather than repeating it with exactly the same words. The speaker can then tell the listener that he or she has it right, or can correct any part of the message that was misunderstood. This also reassures the other person that you are listening and understand them, and that makes most people feel good. A key point is that you don't have to agree with the other people's points of view to give this kind of feedback—all you are doing is letting them know you are listening and understand them. If you disagree or want to present a different way of looking at things, you will have a chance to do so. *Getting and giving feedback to make sure you are communicating clearly can prevent a lot of misunderstandings.* Think about the last time someone didn't listen, totally misunderstood something you were trying to say, and didn't check with you to clear it up. Describe that situation, how you felt, and whether you feel it helped the communication between you and the other person.

_____

_____

_____

i. *Respond to both the spoken and unspoken parts of the message:* As well as giving the other person feedback checking the meaning of his or her words, it is helpful to notice and respond to the feelings he or she seems to be expressing. If others feel we are really paying attention and understanding them, they usually respond favorably. Think about the last time someone noticed your feelings as well as your words; how did they let you know, and how did that lead you to feel?

_____

_____

_____

103

j. *Use a structured communication method:*

(1) Agree to talk about the issue at a time and place that is practical for both people, and that is as free of distraction as possible. If one person wants to talk right away and the other doesn't, agree on a specific time in the near future (how long depends on how much time you have and how big an issue it is).

(2) Agree on who will talk first and who will listen first (you will trade places often, but someone must start).

(3) The first person makes a short statement to the other person, following the guidelines for effective communication—in other words, avoiding fighting words and using this format:

EVENT—RESULT—FEELINGS
"When (event) happened/you did (action), it caused (result), and I felt (feelings)."

Think about a recent time when you were upset with someone, and use this space to write down what you might have said to express your viewpoint in this format.

_____

_____

_____

(4) The first person either agrees that the second person got the message right, or restates any part that was left out or mixed up, or deletes anything that got added.

(5) Trade places and repeat the process. After the first time, you may want to switch to telling one another in plain English what you would like the other person to do or to avoid doing—just say "I would like you to _____." The feedback steps work the same as before.

(6) If you are not willing or able to do what the other person wants, say so in plain English—"I am not willing to _____/I can't _____ because _____." If possible, offer a substitute action, a compromise. Think about the last time someone wanted you to do something you were unable or unwilling to do, and use this space to write how you could have expressed this to the other person.

_____

_____

(7) Keep repeating this process until you feel you are very clear on each other's understandings, feelings, wants, and what you are willing to do for each other.

6. Most of these communication techniques are difficult to remember and practice at first but get easier with practice. It is helpful to practice them with the most important people in our lives, since those are the relationships in which good communication is most important. Part of your homework for this exercise is to talk about this with at least two important people in your life, practice with them, and talk about the results with your therapist and/or your therapy group. Who would be the best people for you to practice these methods with?

_____

_____

7. After thinking about and practicing these communication techniques, what questions do you want to ask your therapist about effective communication?

_____

_____

_____

_____

_____

_____

_____

Remember to bring completed work sheet to your next appointment.

Taking Care of Myself:
Physical and Emotional Self-Care

GOALS OF THE EXERCISE

1. To help the client understand the significance of self-care to recovery efforts.
2. To emphasize that the client can learn to take care of him- or herself with practice.
3. To encourage clients to examine how they spend their time and identify both healthy practices and areas for improvement.

TYPES OF PROBLEMS THIS EXERCISE MAY BE MOST USEFUL FOR

*   Adult Children of Alcoholic (ACOA) Traits
*   Anxiety
*   Appetite Disturbance
*   Borderline Traits
*   Burnout
*   Codependency
*   Depression
*   Emotional Isolation
*   History of Self-Medication for Mood/Pain Problems
*   Inadequate Support Network
*   Medical Issues
*   Post-acute Withdrawal
*   Sleep Disturbance
*   Substance Abuse
*   Substance Dependence
*   Substance Withdrawal
*   Tendency to Repeated Relapse

SUGGESTIONS FOR PROCESSING THIS EXERCISE WITH CLIENT

1. What situations or problems could keep you from following through on your plans for remaining clean and sober?
2. What has gotten in the way of taking care of yourself physically and emotionally in the past?
3. What will happen if you don't follow through on your recovery plans?
4. What will you do in the upcoming weeks to follow through on your plans and take good care of yourself?
5. How will learning to take care of yourself assist your recovery efforts?

TAKING CARE OF MYSELF: PHYSICAL AND EMOTIONAL SELF-CARE

There is a link between taking poor care of oneself and relapsing into substance abuse. When people are abusing alcohol or other drugs, they often neglect basic self-care for both their physical needs (i.e., nutrition, sleep, exercise) and their emotional needs (i.e., safety, competence, sense of value, acceptance, ability to control events around oneself). Your body will heal with abstinence and basic personal self-care in these two areas. This exercise is designed to help you recognize both what you are now doing to take care of yourself and areas where you still have room for improvement.

1. What things are you doing today to take care of yourself physically?

    _____

    _____

2. Physical self-care tracking chart (please keep a record for the next seven days):

Date	*What I planned to do*	*What I did*	*What helped*	*What got in the way*	*How I can overcome in future*
Ex.	Take a walk	No exercise		Procrastinated	Do first thing in a.m.
Ex.	Eat a balanced meal	Ate breakfast	Planned meal		

Date	What I planned to do	What I did	What helped	What got in the way	How I can overcome in future
——	————	————	————	————	————
	————	————	————	————	————
	————	————	————	————	————
——	————	————	————	————	————
	————	————	————	————	————
	————	————	————	————	————
——	————	————	————	————	————
	————	————	————	————	————
	————	————	————	————	————
——	————	————	————	————	————
	————	————	————	————	————
	————	————	————	————	————
——	————	————	————	————	————
	————	————	————	————	————
	————	————	————	————	————
——	————	————	————	————	————
	————	————	————	————	————
	————	————	————	————	————
——	————	————	————	————	————
	————	————	————	————	————
	————	————	————	————	————

3. Please answer these questions about your emotional self-care:

   a. What emotional needs do you have that are not being met today?

   _____

   _____

b. What emotional needs did you try to meet with substance abuse in the past?

_____

_____

c. What methods or resources now help you provide for your emotional needs?

_____

_____

d. What types of emotional pain or deprivation are you able to avoid or cope with?

_____

_____

e. What additional methods or resources do you think you need in order to get your emotional needs met? Where and how can you learn these methods or get these resources?

_____

_____

_____

_____

_____

_____

Remember to bring completed work sheet to your next appointment.

Personal Recovery Planning

GOALS OF THE EXERCISE

1. To help the client begin thinking about recovery as something that involves every aspect of his or her life and that can be approached in a practical way.
2. To prompt the client to think about areas of life where problems may arise, and to help him or her prevent problems by thinking about them in advance or overcome problems more quickly and easily if they do occur later in the recovery process.
3. To help the client create a convenient list of people, groups, and techniques he or she can lean on for support or refer to in times of distress.

TYPES OF PROBLEMS THIS EXERCISE MAY BE MOST USEFUL FOR

- Anger Management
- Anxiety
- Depression
- Emotional Isolation
- Generalized Treatment Resistance
- History of Self-Medication for Mood/Pain Problems
- Impulsivity
- Inadequate Support Network
- Legal Problems
- Learned Helplessness
- Living Environment Deficiencies (Relapse Triggers, Lack of Emotional Support, etc.)
- Low Self-Esteem
- Medical Issues
- Occupational Problems
- Parent-Child Relational Problems
- Partner Relational Problems

111

- Peer Group Negativity
- Poor Social Skills
- Post-acute Withdrawal
- Resistance Based on Distorted Beliefs about Substance Abuse/Dependence
- Substance Abuse
- Substance Dependence
- Tendency to Repeated Relapse
- Treatment/Aftercare Noncompliance

SUGGESTIONS FOR PROCESSING THIS EXERCISE WITH CLIENT

1. How will you begin to implement this plan? What will be the first things you do?
2. What did you learn about your personal recovery process while doing this assignment?
3. Did you have difficulty designing your plan? What was hard? How did you work through it?

PERSONAL RECOVERY PLANNING

> *There are many ways to maintain a healthy lifestyle free of self-defeating behavior. Your recovery plan will be your own creation and will be different from anyone else's. This exercise is meant to give you a starting point and a framework to design your own program. It won't be a finished product when you are done—there will be more questions. It will provide you with a method you can fall back on when things get difficult and confusing.*

1. When you think about your recovery, what do you want to accomplish? Above and beyond staying clean and sober, some things many people want to work toward include control over their actions; self-respect and dignity; peace of mind; the ability to enjoy life; the respect of others; more satisfying relationships; improved health; career progress; and improved financial status. There are many others.

   List the five most important things you want to work on.

   a. _____

   b. _____

   c. _____

   d. _____

   e. _____

2. For each of these items, describe how a return to substance abuse would affect your chances of getting what you want.

   a. _____

   b. _____

   c. _____

   d. _____

   e. _____

3. For each of the things you want to work on, list specifically what you want to accomplish—in other words, how you will know when you've achieved your goals.

    a. _____

    _____

    b. _____

    _____

    c. _____

    _____

    d. _____

    _____

    e. _____

    _____

4. Have you ever tried to cut back or completely quit drinking or using before? _____

    What methods were effective for you, if any?

    _____

    _____

    What methods were ineffective?

    _____

    _____

5. Staying away from using/drinking has two parts: finding *things to do* that work to help you remain abstinent and figuring out which *things not to do* because they may result in returning to use. Drawing on all you have learned so far in your recovery and on the experiences of others, fill out the following:

    a. *Support group activities:* What meeting(s) will you attend during the week? When and where?

    _____

    _____

    When will you meet with your sponsor each week?_____

114

b. *Creating a daily structure and routine:* What things will you do as part of your routine each day, and when will you do them?

_____

_____

Each week? _____

_____

_____

Each month? _____

_____

_____

c. *Basic self-care:* When living compulsively, people often neglect the basics, such as eating a healthy diet, attending to medical needs, getting enough rest, and getting healthy exercise. Incorporating these into your life will increase your ability to cope with stress and relieve stress when it occurs. What are some things you can do in each of the following areas to take care of yourself physically?

Diet:_____

Medical care:_____

Rest: _____

Exercise: _____

d. *Relationships and support systems:* Relationships with loved ones and friends can have a tremendous effect on recovery. You will probably need to assess past and current associations, keep some of these associations in your life, end others, and develop some new relationships that support recovery.

Old relationships: What relationships are likely to support your recovery, and what will you do to strengthen them?

_____

_____

What relationships will probably undermine your efforts, and how will you end or distance yourself from them?

_____

_____

New relationships: Where can you meet people to start some new, healthy, supportive relationships, and how will you go about finding them?

_____

_____

How you can get support from relationships: Please use this space to list names of people you feel you can talk to if you are feeling troubled, confused, or discouraged, and to write about how you will approach each of them to ask for this support.

Name   *How I will ask for support*

_____   _____

_____   _____

_____   _____

_____   _____

_____   _____

e. *Spirituality:* Whether you are religious or not, recovery involves making changes in your values and your goals in life; and people who have spiritual resources to support them are usually more successful in staying clean and sober.

How will you address this component of your recovery?

_____

_____

_____

_____

What questions do you have about this and who can you ask for assistance?

_____

_____

_____

_____

f. *Work:* Your job can be a major source of satisfaction, self-esteem, and security, but also a source of great stress, and recovering people are more likely than average to become workaholics, going overboard on responsibility and burning themselves out.

116

What will you do to keep your work within healthy, moderate limits? _____

_____

_____

_____

_____

How will you deal with it if you find your work is posing a risk to your recovery?

_____

_____

_____

_____

How do you plan on dealing with stress related to work?

_____

_____

g. *Legal issues:* Dealing with the consequences of using and drinking is important in order to avoid undue stress and to gain self-respect.

What are you doing to get any unfinished legal matters settled?

_____

_____

What is one step you can take toward resolving these legal issues today (people to contact; appointments to make; resources needed)?

_____

_____

h. *Finances:* This is also an area that has great impact on self-esteem and stress levels. Many recovering people are intimidated by the financial problems they have when they first quit drinking or using, but find that with determined effort they are able to clear these difficulties up faster than expected.

What financial problems do you have and what are you doing to resolve them?

_____

_____

_____

_____

What is your long-term plan for financial stability?

_____

_____

What is one step you can take today toward resolving these difficulties?

_____

_____

i. *Recreation:* Beginning recovery is a time to renew your involvement in activities you enjoyed in the past or start new activities that you always wanted to try. This will help you cope with stress and increase your enjoyment of life.

List activities you will try or are interested in learning more about:

_____

_____

_____

_____

What steps will you take to incorporate this into your weekly schedule?

_____

_____

What is one step you will take today to work toward having fun?

_____

_____

j. *Other areas of life:* What other things do you see that you should focus on?

_____

_____

_____

_____

What will you do to address these issues?

_____

_____

_____

_____

What is one step you can take today to make progress on one of these issues?

_____

_____

6. *Crisis management:* Your plan needs to include steps to handle any crisis that might trigger a tendency to relapse. Please use this space to list the actions you will take to handle an unexpected (or expected) crisis without relapsing into addictive behavior.

_____

_____

_____

_____

7. *Things not to do because they may lead to drinking or using:* Finally, use this space to list any activities you know you should carefully avoid. This may include going to certain places, seeing some people, or engaging in particular work or recreational activities.

_____

_____

_____

_____

Congratulations! You've created a foundation to build on and a reference that can come in handy in situations where you may be under stress and having trouble thinking clearly. You've now done some of that thinking in advance.

Remember to bring completed work sheet to your next appointment.

Changing Self-Talk

GOALS OF THE EXERCISE

1. To illustrate to clients that what they tell themselves about situations or themselves influences how they feel.
2. To encourage substitution of positive self-talk for negative self-talk to improve self-perception and ability to cope with difficult situations.

TYPES OF PROBLEMS THIS EXERCISE MAY BE MOST USEFUL FOR

*   Adult Children of Alcoholic (ACOA) Traits
*   Anxiety
*   Borderline Traits
*   Codependency
*   Depression
*   Hopelessness
*   Learned Helplessness
*   Low Self-Esteem
*   Mood Swings
*   Post-acute Withdrawal
*   Posttraumatic Stress Issues
*   Shame Issues
*   Substance Abuse
*   Substance Dependence
*   Substance Withdrawal
*   Suicidality
*   Tendency to Repeated Relapse
*   Value Conflicts

120

SUGGESTIONS FOR PROCESSING THIS EXERCISE WITH CLIENT

1. Was this exercise easy or difficult for you? Why?
2. What did you learn about yourself while doing this exercise?
3. How will you use what you learned from this exercise in the next four weeks?
4. An additional adjunct exercise for the client to complete: Pick one positive self-statement. Repeat it to yourself several times every day and visualize how you will demonstrate it throughout the day. Do this daily with the same positive statement for one month and report the results to the group or your clinician.

CHANGING SELF-TALK

All of us have some negative beliefs about ourselves because of experiences or things others have told us that led us to view ourselves negatively. When we talk to ourselves, what we say is often critical and negative. This negative self-talk molds our thoughts, feelings, and actions, and overcoming it takes work. However, when we do this work, we learn to think of ourselves in ways that support our recovery efforts and feelings of self-worth, and that help us eliminate self-destructive behaviors. The purpose of this exercise is to help you identify the harmful messages you give to yourself and increase your ability to replace them with positive self-statements.

1. We all talk to ourselves as we go through the day, either aloud or silently in our thoughts. Over the next week, pay attention to the things you say to yourself, about yourself and your actions. Also, notice when anyone else gives you messages about yourself, such as your boss, coworkers, family members, or friends. When you find yourself saying negative things in your self-talk, or when others are negative or critical toward you, note here what negative messages you repeat to yourself or hear from others most often. Then rewrite them to express your desired situation and self-view in positive terms, and imagine what it would be like to hear these positive messages instead of the negative ones.

	Negative self-statements	*Positive self-statements* *(written in present tense)*
Ex.	I can't stay sober.	I like being clean and sober.
Ex.	I'm weak and this is too hard.	I am learning new skills and getting better.
	_____	_____
	_____	_____
	_____	_____
	_____	_____
	_____	_____

2. Think about a situation in your life now that bothers you. List the negative self-statements that accompany this situation, then describe your feelings when you think about these negative statements and create positive self-statements to replace those negative messages.

Situation: _____

Negative statement	Feelings	Positive replacement statement
_____	_____	_____
_____	_____	_____
_____	_____	_____

3. Does this situation seem more manageable to you after this exercise? If so, in what ways?

_____

_____

4. How can you handle other situations better by using positive self-statements?

_____

_____

_____

_____

Remember to bring completed work sheet to your next appointment.

Setting and Maintaining Boundaries

GOALS OF THE EXERCISE

1. To help clients understand that they have the power to set boundaries for themselves and the right to protect themselves emotionally and physically.
2. To encourage balance and flexibility in relationships where clients may be rigid regarding roles or boundaries.

TYPES OF PROBLEMS THIS EXERCISE MAY BE MOST USEFUL FOR

*   Adult Children of Alcoholic (ACOA) Traits
*   Antisocial Behavior
*   Blaming/Projection/Failure to Take Appropriate Responsibility
*   Borderline Traits
*   Codependency
*   Family Conflict
*   General Interpersonal Relational Problems
*   Issues of Identity
*   Low Self-Esteem
*   Narcissistic Traits
*   Occupational Problems
*   Parent-Child Relational Problems
*   Partner Relational Problems
*   Peer Group Negativity
*   Poor Social Skills
*   Substance Abuse
*   Substance Dependence
*   Unresolved Childhood Trauma

SUGGESTIONS FOR PROCESSING THIS EXERCISE WITH CLIENT

1. When and how in your life did you learn your current beliefs and behaviors about personal boundaries?
2. What roles have alcohol and other drugs played regarding your boundaries in relationships?
3. What is one step for you to take on a daily basis to establish and maintain healthy boundaries?
4. Rehearse how you can cope with resistance and challenges to your boundaries from others in your life: What might they say or do? How might you respond?

SETTING AND MAINTAINING BOUNDARIES

Healthy boundaries in our relationships are permeable—this means we accept people and actions that are positive, helpful, and needed, but protect ourselves from people and actions that are harmful or that interfere with our lives. In trying to protect ourselves, we may keep very rigid boundaries, trusting no one and allowing no one to get close to us emotionally. On the other hand, in our search for love and acceptance we may leave ourselves too vulnerable, becoming too trusting and letting people hurt us too easily. Healthy boundaries protect us. They give us the choice of who we trust, how much we trust those people, and what actions we accept from them, letting us have positive relationships while protecting us from abuse. We also learn to set boundaries on what we do and say to others, respecting their rights as well as our own. This exercise will assist you in evaluating your own boundary system.

1. Make a list of some people with whom you have difficulty setting or maintaining healthy boundaries, along with situations where you have this trouble, and what the results have been for you in the past.

Person	*Situation*	*What happens*	*How you are affected*

2. Are there people, situations, or actions regarding which you are able to set and maintain healthy boundaries? _____ If so, please list them here.

Person	*Situation*	*What happens*	*How you are affected*

3. Why do you think you are able to set and maintain boundaries with the second list of people, situations, or actions, but not with the first list?

_____

_____

4. How can you either use the same methods that work with the second list for the people, situations, or actions on the first list, or use other methods to get the same healthy results?

_____

_____

_____

_____

_____

5. What changes would you like to make in your boundary system to help you live a healthy life?

_____

_____

_____

6. What do you need to do to make these changes?

_____

_____

_____

7. What will you do if others are resistant to accepting your boundaries?

_____

_____

_____

Remember to bring completed work sheet to your next appointment.

Working through Shame

GOALS OF THE EXERCISE

1. To help the client recognize and understand issues of shame and negative self-image.
2. To enable the client to understand connections between negative self-image and substance abuse.
3. To guide the client in building a more positive self-image as part of his or her recovery program.

TYPES OF PROBLEMS THIS EXERCISE MAY BE MOST USEFUL FOR

- Adult Children of Alcoholic (ACOA) Traits
- Borderline Traits
- Codependency
- Family Conflict
- Low Self-Esteem
- Poor Social Skills
- Shame Issues
- Tendency to Repeated Relapse
- Unresolved Childhood Trauma
- Unresolved Grief and Loss

SUGGESTIONS FOR PROCESSING THIS EXERCISE WITH CLIENT

1. Have the client complete this exercise in stages, sharing items as he or she feels comfortable.
2. What evidence do you have for your shaming messages?
3. What connections do you see between shame and your substance abuse?

WORKING THROUGH SHAME

Shame is feeling that as a person, you are bad, inadequate, defective, unworthy, or less than others. It results in feeling hopeless, helpless, and unable to change or succeed. Shame frequently accompanies substance-abusing behavior. There's a difference between guilt and shame. Guilt is feeling that an action is wrong and unacceptable. Shame is feeling that we ourselves are wrong and unacceptable. We can deal with guilt by correcting our actions, but shame is destructive because we can't change who and what we are. If left unresolved, this puts us at high risk of returning to drinking, using, or other self-destructive behaviors. Shame convinces us that we can't get better and don't deserve to feel better. This exercise is meant to help you identify and correct shame in your beliefs about yourself. You deserve to heal!

1. In the first column, please list some mistakes you have made and things you have done wrong as a result of alcohol and other drug use. In the second column, list things you should have done, but didn't do because your drinking or using interfered.

   Mistakes and wrong actions   *Things not done*

   _____   _____

   _____   _____

   _____   _____

   _____   _____

2. What kinds of shaming things do you say to yourself about the things you listed—messages that you are bad, weak, stupid, lazy, evil, or other negative labels?

   _____

   _____

   _____

   _____

3. What messages do you want to repeat to yourself about the things you listed for the first question to replace these shaming messages? (One way to think about this is to ask yourself what you might say to a good friend who was in your situation.)

    _____

    _____

    _____

    _____

4. Each night for the next two weeks, write your answer to the following questions, and talk with your therapist about what you write and any changes you see in your beliefs about yourself: "Of everything I did today, what do I feel the best about? And what kind of person takes that kind of action?"

    Remember to bring completed work sheet to your next appointment.

Section V

Measuring Progress

How Far Have I Come?

GOALS OF THE EXERCISE

1. To reinforce the client's awareness of positive changes he or she has made in sobriety.
2. To help the client plan for further growth and positive change and reinforce self-confidence.

TYPES OF PROBLEMS THIS EXERCISE MAY BE MOST USEFUL FOR

*   Anxiety
*   Depression
*   Generalized Treatment Resistance
*   Hopelessness
*   Issues of Identity
*   Legal Problems
*   Learned Helplessness
*   Low Self-Esteem
*   Peer Group Negativity
*   Post-acute Withdrawal
*   Shame Issues
*   Spiritual Confusion
*   Suicidality
*   Tendency to Repeated Relapse
*   Treatment/Aftercare Noncompliance

SUGGESTIONS FOR PROCESSING THIS EXERCISE WITH CLIENT

1. What areas have you made the most progress in?
2. How are you doing this—how have you made these changes?
3. Have you accomplished things you didn't know you could do? What are they?
4. In what areas do you want to make more changes?
5. How will you make these changes you've identified as goals?
6. In what ways are the changes you've made so far helping your recovery efforts, preventing relapse?

HOW FAR HAVE I COME?

Sometimes it's hard to see the changes we are making. Often change comes gradually and is difficult to measure, and others may see our progress more easily than we can. This exercise is designed to help you identify how you've changed in different areas of your life.

1. Describe how you were thinking, feeling, acting, and coping with difficulties in the following areas of your life _____ months ago.

Area of life	Thoughts	Feelings	Actions	Coping skills
Substance abuse				
Home/family				
Work/school				
Friendships				
Love relationships				
Legal situation				
Finances				
Communication with others				
Self-care				
Leisure activities				
Spiritual life				

2. Now describe how you are thinking, feeling, acting, and coping in the same areas today.

Area of life	Thoughts	Feelings	Actions	Coping skills
Substance abuse				
Home/family				
Work/school				
Friendships				
Love relationships				
Legal situation				
Finances				
Communication with others				
Self-care				
Leisure activities				
Spiritual life				

3. Where do you see the most change?

4. What changes are most surprising for you?

Remember to bring completed work sheet to your next appointment.

Feedback Log:
What Do Others See Changing?

GOALS OF THE EXERCISE

1. To help the client become aware of positive changes he or she has made by using feedback from other people in his or her life.
2. To increase the client's acceptance of and use of emotional support from others.

TYPES OF PROBLEMS THIS EXERCISE MAY BE MOST USEFUL FOR

- Antisocial Behavior
- Borderline Traits
- Depression
- Generalized Treatment Resistance
- Hopelessness
- Issues of Identity
- Learned Helplessness
- Low Self-Esteem
- Peer Group Negativity
- Post-acute Withdrawal
- Shame Issues
- Spiritual Confusion
- Suicidality
- Tendency to Repeated Relapse

SUGGESTIONS FOR PROCESSING THIS EXERCISE WITH CLIENT

1. How do you feel about the feedback you have received?
2. How will you use this information to make other changes?
3. What was the experience of asking for and receiving feedback like for you?
4. How will you use what you've learned to make additional changes?
5. How is the insight you've gained helpful for your recovery efforts?
6. Of all the feedback you heard, what was most surprising for you? What were you happiest to hear?

FEEDBACK LOG:
WHAT DO OTHERS SEE CHANGING?

Sometimes it's hard to measure change in our lives, and feedback from others can help us see our own progress more clearly. This exercise will guide you in gathering feedback from people who are close to you, who will support your recovery efforts, and whom you trust.

1. List 10 people you will ask for feedback about what changes they have seen in your life.

    _____   _____

    _____   _____

    _____   _____

    _____   _____

    _____   _____

2. How will you ask these people about changes they've noticed in you? Think about the questions you will ask. You might want feedback about your relationships, work or school performance, moods, appearance, health, or activities. Use this space to write these question(s).

    _____

    _____

    _____

    _____

    _____

    _____

    _____

    _____

    _____

    _____

    _____

3. Write the feedback you received.

Who I asked   *What they told me*

_____   _____

_____   _____

_____   _____

_____   _____

_____   _____

_____   _____

_____   _____

_____   _____

_____   _____

_____   _____

Remember to bring completed work sheet to your next appointment.

Understanding and Coping with Post-Acute Withdrawal

GOALS OF THE EXERCISE

1. To teach the client about a common syndrome in recovery from chemical dependency that might otherwise lead to demoralization, anxiety, and relapse.
2. To empower the client to cope with post-acute withdrawal and inform him or her of resources and supports available for assistance.

TYPES OF PROBLEMS THIS EXERCISE MAY BE MOST USEFUL FOR

- Anger Management
- Anxiety
- Appetite Disturbance
- Depression
- History of Self-Medication for Mood/Pain Problems
- Hopelessness
- Mania/Hypomania
- Medical Issues
- Memory Problems
- Mood Swings
- Post-acute Withdrawal
- Sleep Disturbance
- Tendency to Repeated Relapse

SUGGESTIONS FOR PROCESSING THIS EXERCISE WITH CLIENT

1. What is it like for you to ask for assistance from others? If you were in their place, how would you feel about being asked for help?
2. How will you use the information you've learned to assist you in maintaining abstinence?
3. How can you remind yourself that this is a temporary problem if you are experiencing symptoms of post-acute withdrawal?

UNDERSTANDING AND COPING WITH POST-ACUTE WITHDRAWAL

Heavy drinking or drug abuse upsets the chemical balance in a person's body. Although it may only take days for alcohol or other drugs to leave the system, the balance can take weeks or months to get back to normal. While this happens, the recovering person may continue to experience physical, mental, and emotional problems. The purpose of this exercise is to help you understand this process if it happens to you and teach you how to get through these problems without relapsing.

1. The symptoms of post-acute withdrawal (PAW) are as follows:

    • Inability to think clearly
    • Low resistance to stress
    • Emotional overreactivity or numbness
    • Memory problems
    • Sleep disturbances
    • Problems with motor coordination

    Have you experienced any of these symptoms since you stopped using alcohol or other drugs? If so, which symptoms have you experienced?

    _____

    _____

2. What methods have you used to try to cope with these symptoms? _____

    _____

    _____

3. Of the methods you've tried, what has worked best for you?_____

    _____

4. Your assignment now is to talk with several other people in recovery and ask them how they have coped with PAW without returning to using/drinking. Who will you ask about this?

    _____

    _____

5. How will you ask them for this information? _____
    _____

6. Based on what you have found works for you and on the experiences of other people, list five things you can do to cope with PAW should you experience symptoms.

    a. _____

    b. _____

    c. _____

    d. _____

    e. _____

    Remember to bring completed work sheet to your next appointment.

Setting and Pursuing
Goals in Recovery

GOALS OF THE EXERCISE

1. To guide the client in formulating his or her own recovery goals.
2. To teach the client general goal achievement life skills to enhance chances of long-term success and quality of life.
3. To increase the client's investment in recovery and encourage him or her to practice these skills outside the treatment setting between sessions and after completion of treatment.

TYPES OF PROBLEMS THIS EXERCISE MAY BE MOST USEFUL FOR

*   Adult Children of Alcoholic (ACOA) Traits
*   Blaming/Projection/Failure to Take Appropriate Responsibility
*   Generalized Treatment Resistance
*   Hopelessness
*   Learned Helplessness
*   Living Environment Deficiencies (Relapse Triggers, Lack of Emotional Support, etc.)
*   Low Self-Esteem
*   Peer Group Negativity
*   Tendency to Repeated Relapse
*   Treatment/Aftercare Noncompliance

SUGGESTIONS FOR PROCESSING THIS EXERCISE WITH CLIENT

1. What benefits will you gain by committing to and following through on this contract?
2. How will accomplishing these goals help you stay clean and sober and prevent relapses?
3. Are the goals you've set realistic in the time frames indicated?
4. Have client and clinician retain a copy of the commitment contract and review progress regularly.

SETTING AND PURSUING GOALS IN RECOVERY

There may be much in our lives over which we have little or no control. This makes it more important that we change whatever patterns we can. In choosing life without alcohol or other drugs, we must make more changes than just quitting drinking or using to support this lifestyle change. This exercise is designed to guide you in setting and achieving goals in recovery.

1. List the changes you want to make in your life, beyond giving up alcohol or other drugs, to support your recovery and avoid relapse. Be sure to list behaviors (things you do), and not characteristics (things you are). Behavior is changeable, while characteristics may not be. For example, people who are shy may not be able to quit being shy, but they can avoid isolating themselves from others by changing the behaviors that kept them isolated. Your goals are:

   Ex. Avoid isolating

   Goal A _____   Goal C _____

   Goal B _____   Goal D _____

2. Now list the methods you will use to achieve your goals. Describe what you will do.

   Ex. Attend three meetings per week; call a friend every day; join a hobby club

   Goal A
   Method 1 _____
   Method 2 _____
   Method 3 _____

   Goal B
   Method 1 _____
   Method 2 _____
   Method 3 _____

Goal C

Method 1 _____

Method 2 _____

Method 3 _____

Goal D

Method 1 _____

Method 2 _____

Method 3 _____

3. The reasons you want to make these changes are: _____

_____

_____

4. The obstacles or barriers that could interfere with your achieving these goals, and the methods you will use to overcome these barriers, are:

Obstacles or barriers	*Methods you will use to overcome*
a. _____	_____
b. _____	_____
c. _____	_____
d. _____	_____

5. The ways other people can help you achieve these goals, and the ways you will get that support from those people, are:

Ways others can help	*Ways you will get their help*
a. _____	_____
b. _____	_____
c. _____	_____
d. _____	_____

6. You will know your plan is working if: _____
    _____
    _____

7. Your therapist and others will know your plan is working if:_____
    _____
    _____
    _____

8. How often will you check your progress toward your goals and make any necessary changes in your methods?
    _____
    _____
    _____

9. When do you plan to finish achieving each of these goals?

    Goal A _____   Goal C_____

    Goal B _____   Goal D_____

10. Fill out a Commitment Contract for each goal you are setting (the form is on the next page). You will sign this contract, as will your therapist and the people who will help you achieve each goal.

    Remember to bring completed work sheet to your next appointment.

COMMITMENT CONTRACT

1. I, _____ , will do the following: _____

   _____

   _____ by this date: _____ .

2. I will take the following actions as my methods to achieve this goal:

   Method 1 _____

   Method 2 _____

   Method 3 _____

3. My supporters, who sign this contract, agree to help me with the following support-ive actions:

   _____

   _____

4. We will meet to discuss my behavior change progress and to confirm support for my behavior change efforts on these dates:

   _____ , _____ , _____ .

5. If I do not make satisfactory progress toward this goal, I will take the following cor-rective action(s):

   _____

   _____

   _____

_____	_____	_____	_____
Your signature	Date	Signature of therapists	Date
_____	_____	_____	_____
Your signature	Date	Signature of therapists	Date
_____	_____	_____	_____
Your signature	Date	Signature of therapists	Date

Section VI

Preventing Relapse

Identifying Relapse Triggers
and Cues: Situations and Feelings

GOALS OF THE EXERCISE

1.   To increase the client's awareness of personal situational triggers and cues to relapse.
2.   To help the client recognize mental, emotional, and behavioral warning signs of relapse.
3.   To guide the client in developing alternative coping strategies to manage relapse triggers, cues, and warning signs.

TYPES OF PROBLEMS THIS EXERCISE MAY
BE MOST USEFUL FOR

- Anger Management
- Anxiety
- Blaming/Projection/Failure to Take Appropriate Responsibility
- Depression
- Family Conflict
- Impulsivity
- Inadequate Support Network
- Living Environment Deficiencies (Relapse Triggers, Lack of Emotional Support, etc.)
- Peer Group Negativity
- Post-acute Withdrawal
- Posttraumatic Stress Issues
- Recent Bereavement/Loss
- Substance Abuse
- Substance Dependence
- Tendency to Repeated Relapse

SUGGESTIONS FOR PROCESSING THIS EXERCISE WITH CLIENT

1. How will you use this information on a daily basis to prevent relapse?
2. What did you learn about your own process of relapse? Do you see any of the patterns described in your own history?
3. Role-play situations in which external pressure to use is high, guiding client in practicing the methods he or she will use to avoid relapse.

IDENTIFYING RELAPSE TRIGGERS AND CUES: SITUATIONS AND FEELINGS

Relapse is common, but it is preventable. Preventing relapse requires awareness of triggers and cues and willingness to do something about it. You have the information that will help you become more aware of situations and feelings that can set you up for relapse. The purpose of this exercise is for you to ask yourself questions so you can become aware of possible relapse triggers and make a plan to cope with them so as to prevent relapse.

Assessing Risky Situations

1. Relapse is often triggered by relapse cues—sights, sounds, and situations that have often been connected with drinking or using in the past. Many recovering people find that unless they are on guard, their thoughts automatically turn back to old behavior patterns when they are around the people with whom they drank or used. Who are the people, or the kind of people, with whom you usually drank or used in the past?

    _____

    _____

    _____

    _____

    _____

2. Because drinking and drug use is often a social activity, you may know people who will expect you to continue to use chemicals with them. They may not understand or care about your need and desire to stay clean and sober, and may use persuasion, teasing, or argument to try to get you to relapse. In your life, who are the people most likely to exert social pressure on you to drink or use? (This list may include all or some of the people you listed in Question 1.)

    _____

    _____

    _____

    _____

    _____

3. Many recovering people find that family members, friends, or coworkers had been enabling their drinking and/or drug use—in other words, these people had helped them avoid the consequences or made it easier in other ways for them to drink and use. Please list here any people who have enabled your drinking or drug use.

_____

_____

_____

4. For each of the people you listed—drinking/using companions, people pressuring you to use, and enablers—please describe how you will avoid relapse triggered by these people's actions.

_____

_____

_____

5. Looking at situations, what are the social situations that you think will place you at greatest risk for relapse?

_____

_____

_____

6. Many people also drank or used drugs to cope with stress, and sometimes relationship issues can be extremely stressful. When you think about your future, how do you think relationship difficulties might put you at risk for returning to drinking or using?

_____

_____

_____

7. For many people, drinking or using had become part of their daily routine, something they did automatically at certain times such as just after work. Reviewing your former daily routines, at what times of the day are you most likely to drink or use?

_____

_____

_____

8. Many people feel the desire to test their ability to maintain recovery in challenging situations, such as being with drinking friends, going to old hangouts, and so on. This often leads to relapse and is an unnecessary risk. In what ways have you tested your ability to stay clean and sober?

_____

_____

_____

9. As another way to guard against stress-induced relapse, please think about both current situations and future life events you need to be prepared to handle without alcohol or other drugs. What are they?

_____

_____

_____

10. What's your plan—what changes are you willing and able to make—to handle the pressures and temptations to drink or use that are associated with the situations you listed?

_____

_____

_____

Assessing Internal Warning Signs

1. When you experience urges or cravings to drink or use, how does your body feel?

_____

_____

2. When you experience urges or cravings to drink or use, what emotions do you usually feel?

_____

_____

3. As mentioned earlier, drinking or drug use is often a tool for coping with stress—in other words, a way to change feelings we dislike to ones we are more comfortable with. What unpleasant feelings will place you at greatest risk for using?

_____

_____

_____

4. Below are some common feelings that people have used chemicals to cope with. It's important not only to be determined not to drink or use in order to cope, but also to know what you will do—not having an alternative to replace substance abuse increases your risk of relapse. Next to each feeling, describe what you will do instead of using to cope with that feeling.

a. Anger _____

_____

b. Anxiety _____

_____

c. Boredom _____

_____

d. Sadness _____

_____

e. Fatigue _____

_____

f. Fear _____

_____

g. Frustration _____

_____

h. Loneliness _____

_____

i. Indifference _____

j. Self-pity _____

k. Shame _____

_____

l. Depression _____

_____

m. Other feelings _____

_____

Remember to bring completed work sheet to your next appointment.

Early Warning Signs of Relapse:
Red Flags

GOALS OF THE EXERCISE

1. To increase the client's awareness of his or her own early warning signs of relapse.
2. To teach the client that relapse is a process and that he or she can prevent that process from continuing to its completion in his or her life.
3. To induce the client to see him- or herself as an active participant in the recovery process.

TYPES OF PROBLEMS THIS EXERCISE MAY BE MOST USEFUL FOR

- Anger Management
- Antisocial Behavior
- Anxiety
- Blaming/Projection/Failure to Take Appropriate Responsibility
- Burnout
- Codependency
- Denial/Rationalization/Minimization of Substance-Abusing Behavior and/or Relapse Risk
- Depression
- Emotional Isolation
- Hopelessness
- Impulsivity
- Inadequate Support Network
- Living Environment Deficiencies (Relapse Triggers, Lack of Emotional Support, etc.)
- Low Self-Esteem
- Mood Swings
- Post-acute Withdrawal
- Substance Withdrawal
- Tendency to Repeated Relapse
- Treatment/Aftercare Noncompliance

SUGGESTIONS FOR PROCESSING THIS EXERCISE WITH CLIENT

1. How will you use this information to prevent relapse? What part of it will be most useful for you personally?
2. Reflecting on past experience, what is the first indicator for you that a relapse may be beginning?
3. What people in your life can help you by telling you if they see warning signs of a relapse in process in your behavior? How can you ask them to give you this help?

EARLY WARNING SIGNS OF RELAPSE: RED FLAGS

> *In addition to external and internal pressures to use, your attitudes, thoughts, and behavior also play a key role in relapse. Changes in attitudes, behavior, feelings, thoughts, or a combination of these could indicate that your relapse process has been set in motion. This exercise will help you identify your personal warning signs. If you can identify the early warning signs, you can prevent relapse from occurring.*

Returning to drinking or using is the completion of the process of relapse, not its beginning. Before a person picks up a drink or drug again, there are normally many warning signs in his or her thinking, attitudes, relationships with others, behaviors, feelings, and moods. Knowing these warning signs can help you cut the process short without returning to substance abuse. In identifying warning signs of relapse, it's helpful to think about the last time you went back to drinking or using after staying clean and sober for a period of time. Doing this will provide you with information about your specific warning signs. It is also useful to ask people who know you well whether they saw any particular warning signs in your behavior, emotions, or thinking. Please think about what possible relapse warning signs you may have experienced yourself or seen in people you know in each of the following areas.

1. Relapse-related changes in thinking may include patterns such as persuading yourself that some new method of being a controlled drinker or drug user will work; remembering the good times and overlooking the problems connected with past substance abuse; thinking of using or drinking as a reward for success; or believing that you cannot succeed in recovery. Please list specific examples of how your thinking changed before your last relapse, or similar changes you've seen in others.

   _____

   _____

   _____

2. Attitudes also change as a recovering person drifts toward relapse. Determination, optimism, teamwork, and motivation may be replaced by negative attitudes such as apathy, negativity, selfishness, and a feeling that being unable to drink is an undeserved punishment. Please list specific examples of how your attitudes changed before your last relapse, or similar changes you've seen in others.

_____

_____

_____

3.   Another area where there are clear differences between the lifestyles of actively addicted people and those of recovering people is in how they relate to others. Before picking up the first drink or drug, behavior toward others usually slips back into addictive patterns, such as self-isolation, manipulation, dishonesty, secretiveness, being demanding and resentful, and putting others after your own wants. Please list specific examples of how your ways of relating to other people changed before your last relapse, or similar changes you've seen in others.

_____

_____

_____

4.   You have probably also seen common behavior patterns in yourself and others who were abusing alcohol or other drugs, and seen very different patterns in clean and sober people. When a person is sliding back toward active use, his or her behaviors usually start looking more and more like they did before abstinence. Some typical addictive behavior patterns include having irregular eating and sleep habits, neglect of health, irresponsibility, reckless high-risk behaviors, procrastination, impulsivity, and others showing a loss of self-control and the growth of chaos in a person's life. Please list specific examples of how your behavior changed before your last relapse, or similar changes you've seen in others.

_____

_____

_____

5.   Together with the other changes described, the feelings and moods of drinking and using people tend to be different from those they experience in recovery. Common addictive patterns of feelings and mood include irritability, anxiety, depression, hopelessness, indifference, self-pity, anger, and self-centeredness. Please list specific examples of how your feelings and moods changed before your last relapse, or similar changes you've seen in others.

_____

_____

_____

6. Now think back, check with others if possible, and identify whatever warning signs preceded your last relapse. If you have never tried to quit before and have no experience of relapse, list the patterns that were normal for you when you were drinking or using. Either way, please write these red flags down in the order in which they happened.

    _____

    _____

    _____

    _____

    _____

    _____

    _____

    After you've completed this exercise, you've gathered the information you need to complete another exercise, "Relapse Prevention Planning."

    Remember to bring completed work sheet to your next appointment.

Putting It All Together: Relapse Prevention Planning

GOALS OF THE EXERCISE

1. To assist the client in developing a plan of action using the information gathered in the previous exercises on relapse triggers and warning signs.
2. To help the client assess his or her commitment to recovery.
3. To teach the client that he or she is responsible for his or her own recovery and can increase the chances of success through planning.

TYPES OF PROBLEMS THIS EXERCISE MAY BE MOST USEFUL FOR

- Blaming/Projection/Failure to Take Appropriate Responsibility
- Denial/Rationalization/Minimization of Substance-Abusing Behavior and/or Relapse Risk
- Emotional Isolation
- General Interpersonal Relational Problems
- Generalized Treatment Resistance
- Impulsivity
- Inadequate Support Network
- Legal Problems
- Living Environment Deficiencies (Relapse Triggers, Lack of Emotional Support, etc.)
- Medical Issues
- Occupational Problems
- Parent-Child Relational Problems
- Partner Relational Problems
- Peer Group Negativity
- Post-acute Withdrawal
- Substance Abuse
- Substance Dependence
- Tendency to Repeated Relapse
- Treatment/Aftercare Noncompliance

SUGGESTIONS FOR PROCESSING THIS EXERCISE WITH CLIENT

1. Have clients put their relapse prevention plans in writing and keep them readily available throughout their daily routines.
2. Have clients present their plans to one another in group and offer critiques and constructive criticism to improve their plans.
3. Who else could give you useful feedback on your plan? Think of people who know you and understand what you are trying to accomplish.

PUTTING IT ALL TOGETHER: RELAPSE PREVENTION PLANNING

If you have done the exercises on relapse triggers and relapse warning signs, you have a good understanding of your own relapse process and how to spot it early on. Now it is time to take this information and design specific techniques to put it to use. The more work you do on this plan and the more specific you are, the more prepared you will be to deal with day-to-day living and unexpected stressful events without reliance on alcohol and other drugs.

1. First, evaluate your thoughts and feelings about sobriety: Are you ready to take any action needed, to go to any lengths to live your life without using mind-altering chemicals? How would you describe your attitude about this?

    _____

    _____

2. What will the consequences be if you return to using alcohol and other drugs?

    _____

    _____

    _____

3. How will you cope if you begin to feel as if you aren't making progress with your recovery, or as if you're backsliding into old drinking and using patterns?

    _____

    _____

    _____

4. Refer to the exercises on relapse triggers and warning signs, or draw on whatever information you have about the process of relapse, and list what you consider your 10 most important personal triggers and warning signs for relapse and what you will do to cope with those triggers and warning signs.

Triggers/warning signs	Specific plan to avoid drinking or using
Ex. Feeling hopeless	Review progress—ask others what change they see
Ex. Urge to use	Attend meetings; contact sponsor; meditate

_____   _____

_____   _____

_____   _____

_____   _____

_____   _____

_____   _____

_____   _____

_____   _____

_____   _____

Work with your therapist, your group, or others to rehearse how you'll handle these situations.

5. Recovery is not a solo process, which is why people who try to quit without help from others usually relapse. Who will you contact for support and assistance? List six people here.

Name	Phone number
_____	_____
_____	_____
_____	_____
_____	_____
_____	_____

6. Emergency planning: Your relapse prevention plan should include what you will do if you encounter a sudden crisis, a stressful situation that triggers a strong urge to use or drink. This plan should be simple and should be something you can start doing right away. If you encounter an unexpected life event that puts you at risk, your plan of action will be:

_____

_____

_____

7. You should also have some general-purpose strategies ready for use if you encounter relapse triggers or warning signs you hadn't specifically planned for. List five general-purpose strategies to stay clean and sober.

_____

_____

_____

_____

_____

8. Changing your routine is important in staying sober. How will you begin and end each day?

_____

_____

_____

9. If your plan includes attending a support group such as Alcoholics Anonymous or Narcotics Anonymous, what meetings will you commit yourself to attend regularly? List those meetings.

Name of group	Day and time	Location
_____	_____	_____
_____	_____	_____
_____	_____	_____

10. Do you foresee any obstacles/barriers to implementing this plan? If so, what are they?

_____

_____

_____

11. What will you do about these roadblocks to your recovery or any others you experience?

_____

_____

_____

12. If your plan isn't enough, and you drink or use again, what will you do to get back on track in your recovery?

_____

_____

_____

13. Are there parts of this plan that you are already carrying out? What are they and how well have they worked?

_____

_____

_____

_____

14. Now that you've got your plan made, it's important to monitor your success in using it and correct it or add to it as needed. When and with whom will you make regular progress checks?

Person   *When you will talk about your progress*

_____   _____

_____   _____

Remember to bring completed work sheet to your next appointment.

Handling Crisis

GOALS OF THE EXERCISE

1. To demonstrate to the client that he or she can handle or prevent crises without using alcohol or other drugs.
2. To encourage the client to plan ahead and find ways to manage a crisis.
3. To provide a written quick reference for the client's use in a crisis.

TYPES OF PROBLEMS THIS EXERCISE MAY BE MOST HELPFUL FOR

*   Adult Children of Alcoholic (ACOA) Traits
*   Anxiety
*   Borderline Traits
*   Codependency
*   History of Self-Medication for Mood/Pain Problems
*   Hopelessness
*   Impulsivity
*   Inadequate Support Network
*   Learned Helplessness
*   Living Environment Deficiencies (Relapse Triggers, Lack of Emotional Support, etc.)
*   Low Self-Esteem
*   Post-acute Withdrawal
*   Posttraumatic Stress Issues
*   Recent Bereavement/Loss
*   Suicidality
*   Tendency to Repeated Relapse
*   Unresolved Childhood Trauma
*   Unresolved Grief and Loss

Suggestions for Processing This Exercise with Client

1. How will this exercise help you in your recovery efforts?
2. How confident do you feel that you'll be able to follow through on this plan if a crisis occurs?
3. What parts of this plan include resources or coping skills you have already used in your life?

HANDLING CRISIS

> *Dealing with unexpected, uncomfortable, and stressful life events is a normal part of living and will occur throughout the recovery process and the rest of our lives. Some crises are preventable, and all crises can be managed without returning to drinking or using. For many people dealing with substance abuse issues, chemicals played a key role in coping with crises; in recovery a crisis can put these people at risk to return to chemical use or drinking. Crisis often evokes feelings of being overwhelmed by intolerable stress. Furthermore, mood swings and emotionality often accompany the early recovery process, making a stressful situation more likely to feel like a crisis. This exercise is designed to help you think ahead today to prevent and/or cope with crisis so that you have a completed quick reference action plan.*

1. A crisis is not usually a total surprise that comes out of nowhere. Often it builds over time, and there are signs that things are beginning to become overwhelming. What signs have you noticed in yourself physically, emotionally, and behaviorally that could tell you that a crisis may be building?

    _____

    _____

    _____

2. Please list three events that you can foresee will be particularly distressing and overwhelming for you, and how you plan to cope with them.

    Event   *Plan*

    _____   _____

                             _____

                             _____

    _____   _____

                             _____

                             _____

    _____   _____

                             _____

3. Often, situations that are easily manageable if we face them early become crises because we procrastinate and neglect to do things we know we will have to do sooner or later—for example, leaving bills unpaid. Are there situations and feelings you are avoiding dealing with or other ways you are setting yourself up for crises?

_____

_____

_____

4. What steps can you take today to prevent crises from building up in your life?

_____

_____

_____

_____

5. Think of someone you know who handles crises well. How does that person do this—what methods and resources does he or she use?

_____

_____

Can you use some or all of the same methods this person employs? If so, which ones? If not, why not?

_____

_____

_____

6. Write the specific steps you will take if you encounter a life event that is so unexpected, uncomfortable, or distressing that it is a crisis for you.

a. _____

_____

b. _____

_____

c. _____

_____

d. _____

_____

e. _____

_____

f. _____

_____

g. _____

_____

h. _____

_____

Remember to bring completed work sheet to your next appointment.

Map of Recovery:
Planning Aftercare

GOALS OF THE EXERCISE

1. To emphasize to the client the importance of self-evaluation and planning in making lifestyle changes that last.
2. To guide the client to attend to successes, thus increasing his or her motivation for continued change.

TYPES OF PROBLEMS THIS EXERCISE MAY BE MOST USEFUL FOR

- Anger Management
- Blaming/Projection/Failure to Take Appropriate Responsibility
- Borderline Traits
- Denial/Rationalization/Minimization of Substance-Abusing Behavior and/or Relapse Risk
- Impulsivity
- Inadequate Support Network
- Living Environment Deficiencies (Relapse Triggers, Lack of Emotional Support, etc.)
- Medical Issues
- Peer Group Negativity
- Poor Social Skills
- Post-acute Withdrawal
- Spiritual Confusion
- Tendency to Repeated Relapse
- Treatment/Aftercare Noncompliance

SUGGESTIONS FOR PROCESSING THIS EXERCISE WITH CLIENT

1. Provide constructive feedback to the client about changes the clinician has observed.
2. How often will you evaluate your successes and check your compliance with your plan?
3. Of all the changes you see in yourself, which means the most to you? To others?

MAP OF RECOVERY: PLANNING AFTERCARE

> *Early in the recovery process, your focus, time, and energy tend to be concentrated on abstaining from substance use. As you accumulate more clean and sober time, your attention will turn to maintaining changes achieved and achieving other personal goals. This exercise has several purposes. First, it is created to help you identify how far you've come and where you are today in your recovery efforts. Second, it is designed to help you identify where you would like to go and how you will get there. It is set up in such a way that you can evaluate and plan at different points in the change process and look toward the future.*

1. *Looking back: Where did you begin?*

    a. What was the date when you took your last drink or drug and decided to quit or entered treatment? _____

    b. What were the main goals you set for recovery that day or during treatment?

    _____

    _____

    _____

    _____

    _____

2. *Taking stock: Where are you today?*

    a. What is the date today? _____

    b. What recovery goals are you now working to accomplish?

    _____

    _____

    _____

    c. What are the primary issues or problems you are addressing?

    _____

    _____

    _____

d. What specific actions and changes are you putting into practice today?

_____

_____

_____

_____

e. What issues do you feel you will need to focus on in recovery during the next year?

_____

_____

_____

_____

f. What relapse trends or self-destructive behavior do you see in yourself today?

_____

_____

_____

_____

g. What successes have you achieved since your last self-evaluation of this kind?

_____

_____

_____

_____

3. *Planning for tomorrow: Where do you want to go from here?*

a. Please write the date when you will next reevaluate your progress. _____

b. What goals do you want to work toward between today and that date?

_____

_____

_____

_____

c. What do you need in order to achieve those goals (information, resources, etc.)?

_____

_____

_____

_____

d. What is the first step you will take after today's self-evaluation?

_____

_____

_____

_____

e. What are the results that will tell you that you are succeeding in these goals?

_____

_____

_____

_____

f. What self-destructive behaviors do you have to watch out for in yourself?

_____

_____

_____

_____

g. Who will you discuss this self-evaluation with (your therapist, your support group sponsor, supportive friends, family members, etc.)?

_____

_____

_____

_____

Remember to bring completed work sheet to your next appointment.

Taking Daily Inventory

GOALS OF THE EXERCISE

1. To identify patterns of thought, emotion, and behavior that pose a threat to the client's sobriety and to guide the client in developing a plan of action for improvement.
2. To clarify for the client the importance of taking inventory as part of preventing relapse.
3. To provide a method for taking inventory for the client to continue using in the future.

TYPES OF PROBLEMS THIS EXERCISE MAY BE MOST USEFUL FOR

- Anger Management
- Antisocial Behavior
- Blaming/Projection/Failure to Take Appropriate Responsibility
- Denial/Rationalization/Minimization of Substance-Abusing Behavior and/or Relapse Risk
- Emotional Isolation
- General Interpersonal Relational Problems
- Generalized Treatment Resistance
- Grandiosity
- Impulsivity
- Learned Helplessness
- Low Self-Esteem
- Narcissistic Traits
- Occupational Problems
- Parent-Child Relational Problems
- Partner Relational Problems
- Peer Group Negativity
- Poor Social Skills
- Substance Abuse

179

- Substance Dependence
- Tendency to Repeated Relapse

SUGGESTIONS FOR PROCESSING THIS EXERCISE WITH CLIENT

1. What was the most important thing you realized about yourself and your actions when you did this exercise?
2. What actions do you think you need to take as a result of what you learned in this exercise?
3. How will that realization help you in your recovery?
4. How will this skill be useful to you in your recovery?
5. How will you use this skill in the future?

TAKING DAILY INVENTORY

> *Your daily emotions, attitudes, and actions, both positive and negative, move you either further into recovery or back toward drinking/using or other self-defeating behavior. Assessing your progress frequently is an important part of maintaining your commitment to change. This exercise will help you identify risk factors and successes early.*

1. Using a rating scale where 1 = low and 5 = high, score yourself daily on the following.

Moving further into recovery	*Moving toward relapse*
____ Honest with self	____ Dishonest
____ Honest with others	____ Resentful
____ Living for today	____ Depressed
____ Hopeful	____ Self-pitying
____ Active	____ Critical of self/others
____ Prompt	____ Procrastinating
____ Relaxed	____ Impatient
____ Responsible	____ Angry
____ Confident	____ Indifferent
____ Realistic	____ Guilty
____ Reasonable	____ Anxious
____ Forgiving	____ Ashamed
____ Trusting of others	____ Fearful
____ Content with self	____ Withdrawn
____ Helpful to others	____ Demanding

2. How did you improve today? _____

_____

_____

3. What roadblock(s) to recovery/progress can you identify today? _____

_____

_____

4. Is there anything you wish you had done differently today? _____

_____

_____

5. What is your level of commitment to recovery/remaining abstinent today? _____
   (Rating)

6. What did you learn about yourself today that you can use to assist continued progress?
   _____

7. Did you begin working on any new changes today? If so, what are they? _____

_____

Remember to bring completed work sheet to your next appointment.

Defense Mechanisms

GOALS OF THE EXERCISE

1. To increase clients' knowledge of the defense mechanisms that interfere with their progress in treatment and ways they have experienced these defense mechanisms in their lives.
2. To point out the benefits and consequences of defense mechanisms.
3. To teach clients about healthier alternative ways to cope with difficulties and the idea that they can learn and use these alternatives.

TYPES OF PROBLEMS THIS EXERCISE MAY BE MOST USEFUL FOR

- Adult Children of Alcoholic (ACOA) Traits
- Anger Management
- Antisocial Behavior
- Blaming/Projection/Failure to Take Appropriate Responsibility
- General Interpersonal Relational Problems
- Generalized Treatment Resistance
- Narcissistic Traits
- Peer Group Negativity
- Poor Social Skills
- Substance Abuse
- Substance Dependence

SUGGESTIONS FOR PROCESSING THIS EXERCISE WITH CLIENT

1. What did you learn about yourself from this exercise?
2. How will you use this information in your recovery?

DEFENSE MECHANISMS

Defense mechanisms are methods people use to defend and protect themselves from uncomfortable, painful experiences and feelings. These mechanisms may save us from short-term distress, but they can be problems when they keep us from looking at ourselves, our world, and our behaviors truthfully. In other words, they can support and maintain self-defeating behavior. This exercise is designed to help you look at how your defenses were created and maintained, how they may be hurting you, and the costs of keeping them.

1. What painful or uncomfortable feelings, thoughts, and situations have you had to deal with during the past year?

    _____

    _____

    _____

2. Some common defense mechanisms include:

    *   Sense of humor
    *   Denial (not being able to see reality)
    *   Projection (seeing other people as having your own problem instead of seeing it in yourself)
    *   Reaction formation (overcompensating by going to the opposite extreme, such as being extra nice to someone you don't like)
    *   Intellectualizing (thinking of situations in nonemotional terms)
    *   Displacement (expressing toward one person or thing what you feel toward another)
    *   Repression ("forgetting" or putting something out of your conscious mind)
    *   Hypochondriasis (thinking you are sick as a way to avoid dealing with a situation)
    *   Sublimation (channeling feelings into safe and acceptable channels, like an aggressive person who plays football)

    What defenses have you used to cope with the feelings, thoughts, or situations you listed for Question 1, and how did you use these defenses?

    _____

    _____

    _____

3. How have your defenses kept you from looking at your alcohol or other drug use realistically?

_____

_____

_____

_____

_____

4. Cost/benefit analysis: Choose one of the defenses that are part of your self-protecting system. What is it? _____ Please complete the following analysis.

Benefits of keeping this defense	_Costs of keeping this defense_
_____	_____
_____	_____
_____	_____
_____	_____
_____	_____
_____	_____
_____	_____

5. How can you become aware as quickly as possible that you are using a defense mechanism?

_____

_____

_____

_____

6. For any defense mechanisms you have decided you want to give up, what will you replace them with to deal with the situations that prompted you to use those defense mechanisms?

_____

_____

_____

_____

Remember to bring completed work sheet to your next appointment.

Addressing Other Disorders Related to Addiction

Dual Diagnosis: Coping with Addiction and Mood Disorders or Bereavement

GOALS OF THE EXERCISE

1. To assist the client in understanding the interaction of chemical dependence and emotional problems or disorders.
2. To reduce relapse by assisting the client in using therapeutic strategies to overcome both chemical dependence and emotional issues.

TYPES OF PROBLEMS THIS EXERCISE MAY BE MOST USEFUL FOR

*   Anxiety
*   Appetite Disturbance
*   Depression
*   Emotional Isolation
*   History of Self-Medication for Mood/Pain Problems
*   Hopelessness
*   Impulsivity
*   Learned Helplessness
*   Living Environment Deficiencies (Relapse Triggers, Lack of Emotional Support, etc.)
*   Low Self-Esteem
*   Mania/Hypomania
*   Mood Swings
*   Post-acute Withdrawal
*   Recent Bereavement/Loss
*   Shame Issues
*   Sleep Disturbance
*   Spiritual Confusion
*   Substance Abuse
*   Substance Dependence

- Suicidality
- Tendency to Repeated Relapse
- Unresolved Childhood Trauma
- Unresolved Grief and Loss

SUGGESTIONS FOR PROCESSING THIS EXERCISE WITH CLIENT

1. How have you used alcohol or other drugs in the past to help you deal with being depressed or suffering from other mood problems?
2. How has your use of alcohol or other drugs led to your being depressed or otherwise mood disturbed in the past?
3. What other activities or situations have helped you cheer yourself up or feel more relaxed?
4. How have you used alcohol or other drugs to cope with grief and loss in the past? What problems did they cause, and what other activities have helped you get over losses?
5. Are there losses or other painful situations you have felt you couldn't handle without alcohol or other drugs? What are they? What is your plan for getting through them clean and sober if they happen?
6. What can others do to help you cope with emotional disorders or grief and loss?

DUAL DIAGNOSIS: COPING WITH ADDICTION AND MOOD DISORDERS OR BEREAVEMENT

Many people suffer from both substance abuse problems and mood disorders such as depression or bipolar disorders. Others find that when they are faced with the death of someone close to them, a divorce, or some other painful loss, they feel they can't cope without alcohol or another drug. This exercise will help you identify and plan for issues of this kind.

What Is the Connection between Substance Abuse and Emotional Issues?

1. People who abuse alcohol or other drugs are more likely to suffer from depression or other mood disorders, and people with mood disorders are at higher risk to have problems with substance abuse. In some cases, they become depressed or manic as a result of their drinking or drug use. Please describe any ways you feel substance use has caused problems with your moods.

    _____

    _____

    _____

2. Sometimes the connection between addiction and moods works in the other direction—the mood problems come first, and when people use chemicals to try to improve their mood they end up getting hooked. Please describe how your mood problems may have led you to drink or use.

    _____

    _____

    _____

3. Many people feel that there are losses or other painful experiences they could not get through without drinking or using. If there are situations you feel would make you relapse, what are they?

    _____

    _____

4. If you know someone who has succeeded in overcoming both addiction and a mood problem or a great loss, how did they do this? Could you use some of their methods? If so, what are they?

    _____

    _____

    _____

5. Many people find that some of the methods they use to overcome chemical dependence, such as participating in recovery programs, learning new coping skills, and finding replacement activities for substance use, also help them with mood problems. What drug and alcohol recovery tools might help you deal with depression, other mood problems, or a serious loss?

    _____

    _____

6. On the other hand, there are some techniques used with mood disorders that may seem not to fit into recovery from substance abuse, such as the use of prescribed mood-altering medications. If you are under a doctor's instructions to take medications for a mood disorder, have you talked about your substance abuse issues with the doctor who prescribed the medications? _____ What did the doctor tell you about this?

    _____

    _____

7. Have you also talked about this with people working with you on your drug or alcohol issues? _____ What did these people tell you?

    _____

    _____

8. If you are participating in a Twelve-Step recovery program, are you aware of the policies such programs have developed about the use of prescribed mood-altering medications? What do you believe those programs have to say about this?

    _____

    _____

9. If you are under a doctor's care and taking prescribed mood-altering medications, what would be the consequences if you stopped taking those medications?

    _____

    _____

    _____

10. Do you know others in a Twelve-Step program who take prescribed mood-altering medications? How do they avoid falling into the trap of substance abuse?

    _____

    _____

11. Please use this space to describe the tools you will use to cope with the combined problems of substance abuse and mood disorders or grief and loss.

    _____

    _____

    _____

    _____

    _____

    _____

Remember to bring completed work sheet to your next appointment.

Dual Diagnosis:
Coping with Addiction
and Posttraumatic Stress Disorder
or Other Anxiety Disorders

GOALS OF THE EXERCISE

1. To assist the client in understanding the interaction of chemical dependence and anxiety disorders.
2. To reduce relapse by assisting the client in using therapeutic strategies to overcome both chemical dependence and anxiety issues.

TYPES OF PROBLEMS THIS EXERCISE MAY BE MOST USEFUL FOR

- Adult Children of Alcoholic (ACOA) Traits
- Anger Management
- Anxiety
- Appetite Disturbance
- Borderline Traits
- Depression
- Emotional Isolation
- General Interpersonal Relational Problems
- History of Self-Medication for Mood/Pain Problems
- Hopelessness
- Impulsivity
- Low Self-Esteem
- Medical Issues
- Mood Swings
- Poor Social Skills
- Post-acute Withdrawal
- Posttraumatic Stress Issues
- Shame Issues
- Sleep Disturbance

- Spiritual Confusion
- Substance Abuse
- Substance Dependence
- Suicidality
- Tendency to Repeated Relapse
- Unresolved Childhood Trauma
- Unresolved Grief and Loss

SUGGESTIONS FOR PROCESSING THIS EXERCISE WITH CLIENT

1. How have you used alcohol or other drugs in the past to help you deal with painful memories, panic attacks, or other problems with anxiety? What other problems did this cause?

2. How has your use of alcohol or other drugs led to your experiencing traumatic situations or feeling anxious or panicky in the past?

3. What other activities or situations have helped you achieve peace of mind and overcome anxiety or emotional pain?

4. What can other people do to help you cope with traumatic or painful memories, feelings of panic, or other problems with anxiety disorders?

DUAL DIAGNOSIS: COPING WITH ADDICTION AND POSTTRAUMATIC STRESS DISORDER OR OTHER ANXIETY DISORDERS

Many people suffer from both substance abuse problems and posttraumatic stress disorder (PTSD), panic attacks, or other anxiety disorders. Others find that when they go through a traumatic experience in recovery, they feel they can't cope without alcohol or another drug. This exercise will help you identify and plan for issues of this kind.

What Is the Connection between Substance Abuse and Anxiety Disorders?

1. People who abuse alcohol or other drugs are more likely than others to suffer from PTSD or other anxiety disorders, and people with anxiety disorders are at higher-than-average risk to have problems with substance abuse. In some cases, they find themselves in traumatic situations as a result of their drinking or drug use. Please describe any ways you feel your substance use has led to your suffering traumatic experiences.

_____

_____

_____

_____

2. Sometimes the connection between addiction and anxiety works in the other direction—the traumatic experiences or other anxiety problems come first, and when people use chemicals to try to cope with the resulting feelings they end up getting hooked. Please describe how your painful experiences may have led you to drink or use.

_____

_____

_____

_____

3. If you know someone who has succeeded in overcoming both addiction and an anxiety disorder, how did they do this? Could you use some of their methods? If so, what are they?

    _____

    _____

4. Many people find that some of the same methods they use to overcome chemical dependence, such as participating in recovery programs, learning new coping skills, and finding replacement activities for substance use, also help them deal with anxiety disorders. What drug and alcohol recovery tools might help you deal with PTSD, panic attacks, or other anxiety disorders?

    _____

    _____

    _____

5. On the other hand, there are some techniques used with anxiety disorders that may seem not to fit into recovery from substance abuse, such as the use of antianxiety drugs and other prescribed mood-altering medications. If you are under a doctor's instructions to take medications for an anxiety disorder, have you talked about your substance abuse issues with the doctor who prescribed the medications? _____ What did the doctor tell you about this?

    _____

    _____

6. Have you also talked about this with people working with you on your drug or alcohol issues? _____ What did these people tell you?

    _____

    _____

7. If you are participating in a Twelve-Step recovery program, are you aware of the policies such programs have developed about the use of prescribed mood-altering medications? What do you believe those programs have to say about this?

    _____

    _____

8. If you are under a doctor's care and taking prescribed mood-altering medications, what would be the consequences if you stopped taking those medications?

_____

_____

9. Do you know others in a Twelve-Step program who take prescribed mood-altering medications? How do they avoid falling into the trap of substance abuse?

_____

_____

10. Please use this space to describe the tools you will use to cope with the combined problems of substance abuse and PTSD or other anxiety disorders.

_____

_____

_____

_____

_____

Remember to bring completed work sheet to your next appointment.

Dual Diagnosis: Coping with Addiction and Thought Disorders

GOALS OF THE EXERCISE

1. To assist the client in understanding the interaction of chemical dependence and thought disorders.
2. To reduce relapse by assisting the client in using therapeutic strategies to overcome both chemical dependence and delusional/hallucinatory symptoms.

TYPES OF PROBLEMS THIS EXERCISE MAY BE MOST USEFUL FOR

*   Anxiety
*   Blaming/Projection/Failure to Take Appropriate Responsibility
*   Denial/Rationalization/Minimization of Substance-Abusing Behavior and/or Relapse Risk
*   Emotional Isolation
*   General Interpersonal Relational Problems
*   Generalized Treatment Resistance
*   Impulsivity
*   Inadequate Support Network
*   Issues of Identity
*   Living Environment Deficiencies (Relapse Triggers, Lack of Emotional Support, etc.)
*   Medical Issues
*   Memory Problems
*   Occupational Problems
*   Parent-Child Relational Problems
*   Partner Relational Problems
*   Poor Social Skills
*   Post-acute Withdrawal
*   Resistance Based on Distorted Beliefs about Substance Abuse/Dependence

- Sleep Disturbance
- Substance Abuse
- Substance Dependence
- Suicidality
- Tendency to Repeated Relapse
- Treatment/Aftercare Noncompliance

SUGGESTIONS FOR PROCESSING THIS EXERCISE WITH CLIENT

1. How have you used alcohol or other drugs in the past to help you deal with frightening or stressful beliefs or delusions, hallucinations, or other problems with disordered thinking? What other problems did this cause?
2. How has your use of alcohol or other drugs led to your experiencing false beliefs or hallucinations in the past?
3. What other activities or situations have helped you achieve peace of mind and overcome the stress of distorted thinking or sensory experiences?
4. What can other people do to help you cope with the hallucinations and/or distorted beliefs you experience with your thought disorder?

DUAL DIAGNOSIS: COPING WITH ADDICTION AND THOUGHT DISORDERS

> *Some people suffer from both substance abuse problems and what are called psychoses or thought disorders, such as paranoid schizophrenia. If you are working to overcome both of these problems, the purpose of this assignment is to help you use the same tools for both tasks where possible, and to guide you in handling some special considerations for this type of dual diagnosis.*

What Is the Connection between Substance Abuse and Thought Disorders?

1. People who abuse alcohol or other drugs are more likely than others to suffer from thought disorders, and people with thought disorders are at higher-than-average risk to have problems with substance abuse. In some cases, they find their thought disorders' beginnings seem to be connected to their drug use, particularly with psychedelic drugs or with prolonged heavy use of stimulants such as methamphetamine. Please describe any ways you feel your substance use has led to your thinking becoming psychotic.

   _____

   _____

   _____

   _____

2. Sometimes the connection between addiction and thought disorders works in the other direction—the hallucinations, false beliefs, or other symptoms of psychosis come first, and when people use drugs (either street drugs or prescription medications) to try to control or cope with these symptoms they become dependent on those drugs. Please describe how your thought disorder's symptoms may have led you to drink or use in the search for relief of those symptoms.

   _____

   _____

   _____

   _____

3. If you know someone who has succeeded in overcoming both addiction and a thought disorder, how are they doing this? Could you use some of their methods? If so, what are they?

    _____

    _____

4. Many people find that some of the same methods they use to overcome chemical dependence, such as participating in recovery programs, learning new coping skills, and finding replacement activities for substance use, also help them deal with thought disorders. What drug and alcohol recovery tools might help you deal with your own thought disorder symptoms?

    _____

    _____

    _____

5. On the other hand, there are some techniques used with thought disorders that may seem not to fit into recovery from substance abuse, such as the use of antipsychotic drugs and other prescribed mind-altering medications. If you are under a doctor's instructions to take medications for a thought disorder, have you talked about your substance abuse issues with the doctor who prescribed the medications? _____ What did the doctor tell you about this?

    _____

    _____

6. Have you also talked about this with people working with you on your drug or alcohol issues? _____ What did these people tell you?

    _____

    _____

7. If you are participating in a Twelve-Step recovery program, are you aware of the policies such programs have developed about the use of prescribed mind-altering medications? What do you believe those programs have to say about this?

    _____

    _____

8. If you are under a doctor's care and taking prescribed antipsychotic medications, what would be the consequences if you stopped taking those medications?

_____

_____

9. Do you know others in a Twelve-Step program who take prescribed mind-altering medications? How do they avoid falling into the trap of substance abuse?

_____

_____

10. Please use this space to describe the tools you will use to cope with the combined problems of substance abuse and schizophrenia or another thought disorder.

_____

_____

_____

_____

_____

Remember to bring completed work sheet to your next appointment.

Dual Diagnosis:
Coping with Addiction and
Other Serious Medical Problems

GOALS OF THE EXERCISE

1. To assist the client in understanding the interaction of chemical dependence and other types of severe medical problems.
2. To reduce relapse by assisting the client in using therapeutic strategies to recover from both chemical dependence and other serious illnesses or injuries.

TYPES OF PROBLEMS THIS EXERCISE MAY BE MOST USEFUL FOR

- Appetite Disturbance
- Depression
- Generalized Treatment Resistance
- History of Self-Medication for Mood/Pain Problems
- Hopelessness
- Inadequate Support Network
- Living Environment Deficiencies (Relapse Triggers, Lack of Emotional Support, etc.)
- Low Self-Esteem
- Medical Issues
- Resistance Based on Distorted Beliefs about Substance Abuse/Dependence
- Substance Abuse
- Substance Dependence
- Substance Withdrawal
- Treatment/Aftercare Noncompliance
- Value Conflicts

SUGGESTIONS FOR PROCESSING THIS EXERCISE WITH CLIENT

1. How have you used alcohol or other drugs in the past to help you cope with severe pain or other symptoms of a serious illness or injury? What other problems did this cause?

2. How has your use of alcohol or other drugs led to your suffering significant injury or illness in the past?

3. What other activities or situations have helped you achieve peace of mind and overcome the pain and stress of your medical problems without drugs?

4. What can others do to help you cope with the pain, stress, and limitations imposed on you by your illness or injury?

DUAL DIAGNOSIS: COPING WITH ADDICTION AND OTHER SERIOUS MEDICAL PROBLEMS

Some people suffer from both substance abuse problems and other medical problems that may be very serious, even life threatening. If you are working to recover from both addiction and another dangerous or intensely painful medical problem, the purpose of this assignment is to help you use the same tools for both tasks where possible, and to guide you in handling some special considerations for this type of dual diagnosis.

What Is the Connection between Substance Abuse and Other Medical Problems?

1. Sometimes there is no connection—it's just coincidence or bad luck that the same person is having a problem with alcohol or another drug and is also badly hurt or sick. However, it's also true that people who abuse alcohol or other drugs are much more likely than others to get hurt or sick, and that people with debilitating injuries are at higher-than-average risk to have problems with substance abuse. In some cases, their injuries or illnesses are directly caused by their drug use. For example, a heroin addict who is infected with hepatitis C through a shared needle is experiencing an illness that would not have happened without his or her drug abuse. Please describe any ways you feel your substance use caused or contributed to your becoming injured or ill.

    _____

    _____

    _____

    _____

2. Sometimes the connection between addiction and medical problems works in the other direction—the life-altering medical crisis comes first, and people try to medicate themselves for their pain or other symptoms and end up with a drug or alcohol problem as well as the injury or disease they started with. When people use drugs (either street drugs or prescription medications) to try to control or cope with their medical symptoms, they may become dependent on those drugs. Please describe how your medical problems may have led you to drink or use in the search for relief of your symptoms.

_____

_____

_____

_____

3. If you know someone who has succeeded in recovering from both addiction and a serious medical problem at the same time, can you understand how they did this? Could you use some of their methods? If so, what are they?

    _____

    _____

4. Many people find that some of the same methods they use to overcome chemical dependence, such as participating in support groups, learning new coping skills, and finding replacement methods and activities for things they can't do any more, also help them deal with injuries or diseases that sharply limit their physical capabilities. What drug and alcohol recovery tools might help you deal with your own medical problems, and how would they help?

    _____

    _____

    _____

5. On the other hand, there are some treatment approaches used for medical problems that may seem not to fit into recovery from substance abuse, such as the use of narcotics and other powerful drugs for pain management. If you are under a doctor's instructions to take medications for your sickness or injury, have you talked about your substance abuse issues with the doctor who prescribed the medications? _____ What did the doctor tell you about this?

    _____

    _____

6. Have you also talked about this with people working with you on your drug or alcohol issues? _____ What did these people tell you?

    _____

    _____

7. If you are participating in a Twelve-Step recovery program, are you aware of the policies such programs have developed about the use of prescribed medications? What do you believe those programs have to say about this?

    _____

    _____

8. If you are under a doctor's care and taking prescribed medications for pain, to prevent infection, or for another valid medical reason, what would be the consequences if you stopped taking those medications?

    _____

    _____

9. Do you know others in a Twelve-Step program who take powerful prescribed medications? How do they avoid falling into the trap of substance abuse?

    _____

    _____

10. Please use this space to describe the tools you will use to cope with the combined problems of substance abuse and a life-altering injury or illness.

    _____

    _____

    _____

    _____

    _____

Remember to bring completed work sheet to your next appointment.

Understanding, Identifying, and Addressing Nonchemical Addictions

GOALS OF THE EXERCISE

1. To assist clients in understanding the essential addictive nature of compulsive behaviors that do not involve use of a drug.
2. To reduce relapse in nonchemically addicted clients by helping these clients apply some of the same techniques they could use for alcoholism or drug addiction.
3. To help clients recovering from substance abuse avoid switching addictions to a behavior that does not involve alcohol or other drugs but may be equally disruptive to the lives of these clients and their friends and loved ones.

TYPES OF PROBLEMS THIS EXERCISE MAY BE MOST USEFUL FOR

*   Adult Children of Alcoholic (ACOA) Traits
*   Anxiety
*   Blaming/Projection/Failure to Take Appropriate Responsibility
*   Borderline Traits
*   Burnout
*   Codependency
*   Depression
*   Emotional Isolation
*   Family Conflict
*   General Interpersonal Relational Problems
*   Generalized Treatment Resistance
*   Grandiosity
*   Hopelessness
*   Impulsivity
*   Inadequate Support Network
*   Learned Helplessness

- Living Environment Deficiencies (Relapse Triggers, Lack of Emotional Support, etc.)
- Low Self-Esteem
- Narcissistic Traits
- Occupational Problems
- Parent-Child Relational Problems
- Partner Relational Problems
- Poor Social Skills
- Resistance Based on Distorted Beliefs about Substance Abuse/Dependence
- Shame Issues
- Spiritual Confusion
- Tendency to Repeated Relapse
- Treatment/Aftercare Noncompliance
- Value Conflicts

SUGGESTIONS FOR PROCESSING THIS EXERCISE WITH CLIENT

1. How have you used habit-forming behaviors that didn't include alcohol or other drugs to cope with life or change your mood in the past? What other problems did this cause?
2. How has your engaging in this behavior affected your relationships with your family and friends?
3. What other activities or situations have helped you achieve peace of mind and feel good, or overcome the pains and stresses of life, without becoming compulsive?

UNDERSTANDING, IDENTIFYING, AND ADDRESSING NONCHEMICAL ADDICTIONS

Some people suffer from addictions that don't seem to fit the standard definition. A person might be thoroughly addicted, be just as unable to control his or her use of a behavior as any alcoholic or addict who is unable to stop drinking or using, and lose most of the same things—relationships, jobs, self-respect, money, and so on. Yet this person might never have taken a drug stronger than children's aspirin and never drunk anything stronger than root beer. Newly recovering alcoholics and addicts are at especially high risk for becoming addicted to other behaviors without realizing at first that it is happening. The goal of this assignment is to increase your awareness of this danger and suggest some tools you can use to avoid it or overcome it.

What Is the Connection between Substance Abuse and Nonchemical Addictions?

1. Nonchemical additions are also called compulsive behaviors, and people do the things they get hooked on for the same reasons they use alcohol or other drugs—to make them feel better, to help them cope with a situation or solve a problem, or to impress others and gain or maintain social status. Can you think of a time when you started out doing something to feel good, accomplish a task, or make an impression, and got so carried away you lost control and weren't able to stop when you meant to?

    _____

    _____

    _____

2. What kinds of activities came to mind for you when this subject was introduced? Many people think first of compulsive gambling; if you did, start your answer with that, then add whatever other activities you thought of.

    _____

    _____

    _____

3. If you know someone who has succeeded in recovering from a nonchemical addiction, can you understand how they did this? Did they use any of the same methods you are using for alcohol or other drugs?

_____

_____

4. Where the methods are different, could you use some of these people's techniques either for the same problem they are working on or for other problems in your own life? If so, what are they?

_____

_____

5. Many people find that some of the same methods that can be used to overcome chemical dependence, such as participating in support groups, learning new coping skills, and finding replacement methods and activities for things they can't do any more, also help them deal with compulsive behaviors outside the realm of drinking and using. This isn't a new idea. After all, as those who are involved with Alcoholics Anonymous or another Twelve-Step program soon learn, the idea is "to practice these principles in all our affairs." What drug and alcohol recovery tools might help you deal with your own medical problems, and how would they help?

_____

_____

_____

6. Have you also talked about this with people working with you on your drug or alcohol issues? _____ What did these people tell you?

_____

_____

7. If you are participating in a Twelve-Step recovery program, are you aware of the policies such programs have developed about addressing other issues in meetings? Some groups are much more open and accepting of a variety of topics than others. What do you believe your group's policy is about this?

_____

_____

8.   Please use this space to describe the methods and sources of support you will use to cope with any addictive problem not involving alcohol or other drugs that you might have now or might develop someday.

_____

_____

_____

_____

_____

Remember to bring completed work sheet to your next appointment.

Understanding, Identifying, and Addressing Codependent Behaviors

GOALS OF THE EXERCISE

1. To assist the client in understanding the essential addictive nature of codependency and addictive relationships.
2. To reduce the incidence of newly recovering clients becoming involved in codependent relationships that jeopardize their sobriety.
3. To help the friends and families of clients in treatment to understand how they can help the clients and themselves by avoiding the trap of codependent behaviors.

TYPES OF PROBLEMS THIS EXERCISE MAY BE MOST USEFUL FOR

- Adult Children of Alcoholic (ACOA) Traits
- Anger Management
- Anxiety
- Blaming/Projection/Failure to Take Appropriate Responsibility
- Borderline Traits
- Burnout
- Codependency
- Denial/Rationalization/Minimization of Substance-Abusing Behavior and/or Relapse Risk
- Depression
- Emotional Isolation
- Family Conflict
- Generalized Treatment Resistance
- Grandiosity
- Living Environment Deficiencies (Relapse Triggers, Lack of Emotional Support, etc.)
- Low Self-Esteem
- Parent-Child Relational Problems

213

- Partner Relational Problems
- Shame Issues
- Unresolved Childhood Trauma
- Unresolved Grief and Loss
- Value Conflicts

SUGGESTIONS FOR PROCESSING THIS EXERCISE WITH CLIENT

1. Could you state in your own words what the word *codependent* means to you?
2. How have you seen people you knew affected by codependence in their relationships?
3. How can you and any members of your family affected by codependence help each other overcome both the chemical problem and the behavior problem?

UNDERSTANDING, IDENTIFYING, AND ADDRESSING CODEPENDENT BEHAVIORS

> Codependency *is a word meaning "addiction to a person or relationship." The easiest way to describe it is to say that a codependent is working so hard at trying to control and "fix" someone else that his or her own life is in turmoil as a result. This is another trap that waits for newly clean and sober alcoholics and addicts; we want to rescue people who don't seem to know they need help. Since no one can control another person's thoughts, feelings, or behavior, the codependent person is setting him- or herself up for one painful disappointment after another. This assignment is meant to help you avoid falling into this trap in your recovery.*

Why Do People Get Involved in Addictive Relationships?

1. There are several reasons people get drawn into codependent or addictive relationships where they are trying harder to straighten others out than those others are trying themselves. Please remember the definition given in the introduction, and think about your own relationship history. Did you get into, or stay in, any relationships with addicted or abusive partners? If you did, do one or more of these reasons help explain why? Check any that fit.

    __ You felt needed.

    __ It was intense and exciting from the start.

    __ You just naturally felt drawn to them.

    __ They made you feel strong and smart and capable.

    __ The sex was incredible.

    __ You identified with the hardships they'd suffered.

    __ You felt you could help them and change their life.

    __ You felt sorry for them.

    __ You couldn't say no.

2. If you have gotten into relationships for these reasons, how have they usually turned out?

   _____

3. What is happening in a codependent relationship is that the two people are using each other to try to make themselves feel the way they want to feel, just as they would use a drug. The telltale signs of a codependent relationship are clear, and if these people weren't so emotionally involved, they could easily see that something was wrong. Here are signs of an addictive or codependent relationship. Again, please check off any that apply in your own experience.

   __ Manipulation and mind games take up a lot of time and energy.

   __ Either you, your partner, or both are often anxious and worried that the relationship will break up, so you spend much of your time "walking on eggshells" to avoid this.

   __ You tend to keep your partner away from your other friends and family because they don't get along very well, or you don't think they would.

   __ One of you spends a lot of time and effort rescuing the other from problems over and over again.

   __ You work hard at impressing each other and keep many secrets about yourselves because you fear your partner would reject you if he/she knew about some parts of your life.

   __ You get in heated arguments that don't make sense to either of you.

   __ The relationship became very intense very fast when you first got together.

   __ One or both of you feel a lot of jealousy and insecurity about the relationship.

   __ The relationship is never boring, but it's always stressful.

   __ You go back and forth between feeling abandoned and feeling smothered.

4. Again, if you have gotten into this type of relationship, how has it usually turned out?

   _____

5. Looking over the items you have checked off, if you've been in one of these relationships, does this look like a description of a highly stressful situation? _____ As you may know, there is a connection between stress and relapse into addiction. First, think back to when you first started drinking or using. Was relief of stress one of the reasons? If it was, do you think this kind of relationship could make a person more prone to relapse into alcohol or drug use? What are your thoughts on that idea?

   _____

   _____

216

6. Most people who get into codependent relationships don't do so only one time. Each individual has a pattern, a certain type of person he or she finds most attractive. If you are the kind of person who unconsciously expects the type of relationship described, the potential partners who would form that kind of relationship with you (of course, you would be doing the same things) are the people you're most attracted to. If they're codependent types, then if you're codependent you'll probably be most attractive to them too. Have you had experiences where you met someone and you couldn't seem to take your eyes off them, and the attraction was mutual? Please use this space to write about that situation and what happened in the relationship over time.

   _____

   _____

7. So now that you've noticed and studied this problem, what can you do about it? What ideas for solutions come to mind at this moment?

   _____

   _____

   _____

8. There are a variety of resources available to help people avoid codependent relationships or try to change them into healthy ones. If you have already seen or heard of any of these resources, please write whatever information you have about them here.

   _____

   _____

   _____

   _____

9. Just as is true for alcoholism and addiction, there are many books and films that describe the problems of codependency well and give examples, then go on to recommend ways to change these unsatisfying relationships into healthy ones. Your therapist can probably suggest some, and your local library should have those books and possibly films for your use. What are some books and films you know of that tell stories about codependent relationships?

   _____

   _____

217

10. As with alcohol and other drugs, once you've identified the problem and you understand it at least somewhat, you don't have to work on it alone. If you're concerned about co-dependency in your relationships, let your therapist know, and he or she can provide you with a lot of information and tools to use. Have you asked your therapist about working on this issue in your therapy? What was his or her response? What work would you like to do with this in therapy—what goal would you set? What change in your life would you like to happen? And how do you think changing the way you act in your relationships will affect your chances of staying clean, sober, and happy?

_____

_____

_____

_____

Remember to bring completed work sheet to your next appointment.

Section VIII

Specific Assignments for Work with Twelve-Step Programs

Twelve-Step Meeting Review/
Critique Form

GOALS OF THE EXERCISE

1. To assess the client's participation and areas of attention in attending Twelve-Step meetings.
2. To prompt the client to identify similarities between his or her experiences and those of others at meetings.
3. To identify areas of confusion or resistance related to Twelve-Step meetings for therapeutic attention.
4. To suggest types or formats of meetings most likely to be accepted by the client.

TYPES OF PROBLEMS THIS EXERCISE MAY BE MOST USEFUL FOR

- Adult Children of Alcoholic (ACOA) Traits
- Anxiety
- Blaming/Projection/Failure to Take Appropriate Responsibility
- Codependency
- Denial/Rationalization/Minimization of Substance-Abusing Behavior and/or Relapse Risk
- Depression
- Emotional Isolation
- General Interpersonal Relational Problems
- Generalized Treatment Resistance
- Grandiosity
- Hopelessness
- Impulsivity
- Inadequate Support Network
- Issues of Identity
- Learned Helplessness
- Low Self-Esteem
- Narcissistic Traits

- Peer Group Negativity
- Poor Social Skills
- Post-acute Withdrawal
- Resistance Based on Distorted Beliefs about Substance Abuse/Dependence
- Resistance Based on Distorted Beliefs about Support Groups
- Shame Issues
- Spiritual Confusion
- Substance Abuse
- Substance Dependence
- Substance Withdrawal
- Tendency to Repeated Relapse
- Treatment/Aftercare Noncompliance
- Value Conflicts

SUGGESTIONS FOR PROCESSING THIS EXERCISE WITH CLIENT

1. What other kinds of meetings have you attended?
2. What kind of meeting do you think would be the best fit for you?
3. Were there people who seemed more different from you than they turned out to be when they talked about their lives?
4. If you had talked about your experiences related to this topic, what might you have said?

TWELVE-STEP MEETING REVIEW/ CRITIQUE FORM

Do not take this form to a meeting with you, and do not write information that would violate anyone's anonymity or confidentiality.

---

1. Meeting information:

    Program (A.A., N.A., etc.): _____   Location: _____   Date/time: _____

    Meeting format: ( ) Tag/open sharing   ( ) Speaker meeting   ( ) Big Book/Step study

    ( ) All male/all female   ( ) Young people's   ( ) Other _____

2. What was the main topic of the meeting?

    _____

3. What were your general thoughts and feelings on that topic?

    _____

    _____

4. In what ways could you relate to the experiences and feelings shared by others at the meeting? Were you unable to relate to some people, and if so, what was the difference between them and you that made you unable to relate?

    _____

    _____

    _____

5. What other thoughts and feelings did this meeting cause you to have?

    _____

    _____

6. What did you gain from this meeting?

    _____

Remember to bring completed work sheet to your next appointment.

Understanding Spirituality

GOALS OF THE EXERCISE

1. To overcome client resistance to Twelve-Step programs based on antipathy toward religion.
2. To broaden the client's understanding of spirituality and how it applies to overcoming addictions.

TYPES OF PROBLEMS THIS EXERCISE MAY BE MOST USEFUL FOR

-   Adult Children of Alcoholic (ACOA) Traits
-   Anxiety
-   Denial/Rationalization/Minimization of Substance-Abusing Behavior and/or Relapse Risk
-   Depression
-   Emotional Isolation
-   Generalized Treatment Resistance
-   Grandiosity
-   Hopelessness
-   Impulsivity
-   Inadequate Support Network
-   Issues of Identity
-   Learned Helplessness
-   Low Self-Esteem
-   Narcissistic Traits
-   Peer Group Negativity
-   Resistance Based on Distorted Beliefs about Support Groups
-   Shame Issues
-   Spiritual Confusion
-   Substance Abuse

- Substance Dependence
- Substance Withdrawal
- Tendency to Repeated Relapse
- Treatment/Aftercare Noncompliance
- Value Conflicts

SUGGESTIONS FOR PROCESSING THIS EXERCISE WITH CLIENT

1. What have you thought or heard about spirituality in the past?
2. How much of what you had learned in the past was different from the ideas in this exercise?
3. Did this exercise change your understanding of Twelve-Step groups and how they work?
4. How can you use a focus on spirituality to help you overcome the problem?

UNDERSTANDING SPIRITUALITY

This assignment is designed to help you begin working through an issue that troubles many people new to recovery programs—the issue of spirituality. This is a big subject, and there is no way one handout like this can cover it all, but we can offer you some pointers to get you started.

Why work on spirituality? Because it can make the difference between success or failure in staying clean and sober. It is the key to effective use of Alcoholics Anonymous (A.A.), Narcotics Anonymous (N.A.), and other Twelve-Step programs.

When people attend their first Twelve-Step program meetings and find they dislike these programs, the most common reason is that they are uncomfortable with all the talk about God. This may look like a barrier that makes these programs useless to them. This doesn't have to be true.

Many people, and especially those who have problems with alcohol or other drugs, have good reasons to feel skeptical about religion. They may have had bad experiences with religious people or institutions. Perhaps they just feel that God has not been there when they needed Him. Hearing God or a Higher Power mentioned in seven of the Twelve Steps may be an immediate turn-off.

However, many people who considered themselves atheists or agnostics, who either definitely did not believe in God or believed that no one could know for certain whether God exists, have found that they can use A.A., N.A., and other Twelve-Step programs to make the changes they want to make in their lives. *The key is understanding the difference between spirituality and religion.*

1. Please write down your description of religion—what you think of when you hear the word.

    _____

    _____

2. Now think about the word *spirituality,* and write your definition for this word.

    _____

    _____

3.   Are there differences in the meanings of religion and spirituality for you? _____ If so, what is the biggest difference you see?_____

_____

A dictionary definition of *religion* could go like this:

> A religion is a specific system of practices and rituals, based on a belief in a specific divine or superhuman power, usually practiced through membership in a specific human organization, usually called a church.

A similar definition for *spirituality,* on the other hand, might sound like this:

> Spirituality is a focus on the moral aspects of life, on what is right and will help us become the best people we are capable of being.

We could say it this way: A religion is a way created by people to try to achieve spirituality. We could think of spirituality as like water and religion as like a bottle, a container to hold water—water can exist outside of a bottle, and some bottles contain other things instead of water.

4.   Does this idea make sense to you? _____ What other "containers" for spirituality can you think of—other ways to help yourself focus on what is right in life?

_____

_____

5.   At this point, you may be thinking, "Doesn't this definition of religion also describe a Twelve-Step program? It seems to be a specific system of practices and rituals, and it is practiced through membership in a specific organization!" Have you had the thought that A.A., N.A., or some other Twelve-Step program seemed to resemble a church? If so, what similarities do you see?

_____

_____

6.   What differences do you see between Twelve-Step groups and churches?

_____

_____

Here are three key differences between Twelve-Step groups and churches:

- *Specific definitions of God:* A church or religion offers specific ways to understand God, and may insist no other way can be correct. A Twelve-Step program asks you to think in terms of a power greater than yourself, and leaves it up to you to decide what that power is and how it works.

- *Authority:* While a church normally has a formal hierarchy and structure of people in charge, in a Twelve-Step group nobody is in charge. There is no chain of command. Decisions are made by the group through a vote called a group conscience.
- *Membership requirements:* Religions may restrict their membership in many ways—by birth, heritage, or obedience to various rules. By contrast, in any Twelve-Step program, the Third Tradition says that the only membership requirement is a desire to solve the problem that group exists to overcome. Anyone who wants to be a member can do so, and no one can be excluded.

7. How might these differences might make a Twelve-Step program work differently from a church?

_____

_____

_____

8. Going back to our definition of spirituality, how do you think paying attention to the moral aspects of life and what is right could help you solve the problems facing you with alcohol, other drugs, or other addictive behaviors?

_____

_____

_____

If you see that a focus on these parts of your life could be useful, that's all it takes to begin including spirituality in your recovery work.

Remember to bring completed work sheet to your next appointment.

Step One:
Understanding Powerlessness

GOALS OF THE EXERCISE

1. To enable the client to break through denial and identify instances in which his or her substance use or other compulsive behavior has gotten out of control.
2. To normalize the experience of powerlessness to reduce the client's sense of isolation.
3. To show the client that others have overcome similar problems to increase his or her sense of hope and empowerment.
4. To help the client begin working the Twelve Steps.

TYPES OF PROBLEMS THIS EXERCISE MAY BE MOST USEFUL FOR

- Adult Children of Alcoholic (ACOA) Traits
- Anger Management
- Anxiety
- Blaming/Projection/Failure to Take Appropriate Responsibility
- Codependency
- Denial/Rationalization/Minimization of Substance-Abusing Behavior and/or Relapse Risk
- Depression
- Emotional Isolation
- Family Conflict
- General Interpersonal Relational Problems
- Generalized Treatment Resistance
- Grandiosity
- Hopelessness
- Impulsivity
- Inadequate Support Network
- Issues of Identity
- Learned Helplessness

- Low Self-Esteem
- Narcissistic Traits
- Occupational Problems
- Parent-Child Relational Problems
- Partner Relational Problems
- Peer Group Negativity
- Poor Social Skills
- Post-acute Withdrawal
- Resistance Based on Distorted Beliefs about Substance Abuse/Dependence
- Resistance Based on Distorted Beliefs about Support Groups
- Shame Issues
- Spiritual Confusion
- Substance Abuse
- Substance Dependence
- Substance Withdrawal
- Tendency to Repeated Relapse
- Treatment/Aftercare Noncompliance
- Unresolved Grief and Loss
- Value Conflicts

SUGGESTIONS FOR PROCESSING THIS EXERCISE WITH CLIENT

1. What are some areas of life where you see that all human beings are powerless?
2. Did examining the effect of powerlessness on someone you admire change the way you feel about this issue?
3. How did your understanding of your own life change when you did this exercise?
4. How did your feelings about Twelve-Step groups change when you did this exercise?

STEP ONE: UNDERSTANDING POWERLESSNESS

> *This assignment is designed to help you work your First Step in your Twelve-Step program. If you have already worked Step One, please use this workbook to record the answers you found to these questions when you worked that Step. It would be a good idea to go through this workbook with your therapist and your Twelve-Step program sponsor.*

Am I Powerless? What Does Powerlessness Mean to Me?

We have a difficult time accepting that we can't control things we thought we could control—especially if other people are not powerless in these areas. Some of the things we may be powerless over are alcohol and other drugs, other people and their actions, compulsive behaviors such as gambling, spending money, or overeating, or even our own feelings at times.

The idea that we might be powerless is both unpleasant and hard to believe for many of us. However, if we really are powerless, denying it does not improve our lives. It just leaves us off guard and less able to avoid danger or pain. Step One helps us see ourselves and the world around us more realistically, to stop stumbling into pitfalls because we can't see them under our feet.

Powerlessness doesn't have to be constant—losing control once in a while may be all it takes to make our lives unmanageable.

Many people trying to understand what has happened because of their use of alcohol and other drugs, or because of other compulsive behavior, start out with ideas about powerlessness that don't fit them, and convince themselves they can't be powerless. Look over the following statements and check any that sound like things you may have been saying or thinking.

___ If I were powerless, I'd be drinking or using all the time—I only drink at certain times (on weekends, at night, at home, out of town, etc.), so I can't be powerless!

___ If I were powerless, I'd be unable to stop once I started every time I drank/used/did that—some/most of the time, I can stop when I want to, so I can't be powerless!

___ If I were powerless, I'd be homeless, unable to hold a job, unable to take care of my kids, unable to pay my bills, and so on—I function pretty well and do what's expected of me, so I can't be powerless!

___ If I were powerless, I'd be getting in trouble, getting DUIs, and so on—I've never been in trouble connected with this, so I can't be powerless!

It may help to consider it this way. Suppose you were shopping for a used car, and a salesperson showed you a nice-looking car and said to you: *This one's a lot of fun, and the steering wheel and the brakes work most of the time. Once in a while it won't go where you try to steer it, and every now and then it doesn't stop when you hit the brake pedal—but nine times out of ten, the controls work just fine.*

Would you buy that car, or would you feel it was unsafe?

If a driver were powerless over his or her car one time in a hundred, most of us would feel that was enough powerlessness to be a serious problem.

If we are powerless over what happens when we drink or use or take some other action one time in a hundred, we are powerless over it. If we are powerless to keep ourselves from doing anything one time in a hundred, we are powerless over it.

1. Please read through the following, and check any items that are true in your life.

    ___ I have done something while drinking/using/engaging in this behavior that I didn't mean to do, or that I definitely meant not to do.

    ___ I have found myself drinking/using/engaging in this behavior when I didn't plan to do so and had said I wouldn't.

    ___ I have found myself drinking/using/engaging in this behavior more, or for longer, than I planned when I started.

2. Describe two times when you lost control with alcohol, another drug, or a problem behavior.

    _____

    _____

3. Give examples of things you have done because of these losses of control that were bad for your health, your career, your relationships, or other important parts of your life.

    _____

    _____

4. Give examples of ways you have tried to control this situation in your life.

    _____

    _____

5. How do you feel about the idea that you are powerless in this matter?

    _____

6. Many feel it's not okay to be powerless. Alcoholics and addicts in particular tend to be their own harshest judges. Give examples of negative judgments you have made of your-

self because of your inability to control your actions around this substance or behavior in your life.

_____

_____

7. Part of addiction is that our unwillingness to face this powerlessness, and our harsh judgment of ourselves, make us dishonest with ourselves and others. We lie about our actions, motives, thoughts, and feelings, because it would be too uncomfortable to admit the truth. This dishonesty spreads to other parts of our lives. Give examples of dishonesty in your life.

_____

_____

8. How has the deceptive behavior you described worked in your life—what were the results?

_____

_____

9. What would happen if you were honest with yourself and others about these things?

_____

_____

10. Think of other people you have known who have done some of the same kinds of things. How were you affected by their dishonesty?

_____

_____

11. The other side of powerlessness is lack of responsibility. If we have no power over a thing, we can't be responsible for it. When we deny our powerlessness, we feel responsible for things we don't control. What are things you feel responsible for that you don't have any control over?

_____

_____

12. How has feeling responsible for these things affected your life?

_____

_____

13. What would happen if you stopped trying to control these things?

_____

_____

14. Many people feel that powerlessness means that we have no responsibility for anything, that it is a cop-out. Are there things you really are responsible for that you have blamed on other people or things outside yourself? If so, what are some of them?

_____

_____

15. How has your holding others responsible for these things affected your life?

_____

_____

16. How would your life be affected if you accepted responsibility for these things?

_____

_____

17. Think of someone for whom you have great respect. What are some things that person is powerless over, and how has he or she handled that powerlessness?

_____

_____

18. Often, when we see someone accept the unchangeable with calm and serenity, it increases our respect for them. Does the powerlessness of that person in the areas you just mentioned reduce the respect you and others have felt for him or her?_____

19. Now do an exercise in imagination: Picture yourself in the future, living a life in which you are honest with yourself and others about what you have power over, what you're powerless over, and what choices and actions you're responsible for. How would others feel about you? How would you feel about yourself? Please write a short description of how you think this life would be different from your life now, and talk about this with your therapist and your sponsor.

_____

_____

_____

_____

_____

_____

Remember to bring completed work sheet to your next appointment.

Step Two: Finding Hope

GOALS OF THE EXERCISE

1. To assist the client in continuing to work the Twelve Steps.
2. To assist the client in identifying spiritual issues for therapeutic work.
3. To increase the client's awareness of ways Twelve-Step programs can be adapted to fit his or her value system.
4. To begin addressing spiritual issues that may interfere with success in recovery.

TYPES OF PROBLEMS THIS EXERCISE MAY BE MOST USEFUL FOR

*   Adult Children of Alcoholic (ACOA) Traits
*   Anger Management
*   Anxiety
*   Blaming/Projection/Failure to Take Appropriate Responsibility
*   Codependency
*   Denial/Rationalization/Minimization of Substance-Abusing Behavior and/or Relapse Risk
*   Depression
*   Emotional Isolation
*   Generalized Treatment Resistance
*   Grandiosity
*   Hopelessness
*   Impulsivity
*   Inadequate Support Network
*   Issues of Identity
*   Learned Helplessness
*   Low Self-Esteem
*   Narcissistic Traits
*   Peer Group Negativity

- Poor Social Skills
- Post-acute Withdrawal
- Resistance Based on Distorted Beliefs about Substance Abuse/Dependence
- Resistance Based on Distorted Beliefs about Support Groups
- Shame Issues
- Spiritual Confusion
- Substance Abuse
- Substance Dependence
- Substance Withdrawal
- Tendency to Repeated Relapse
- Treatment/Aftercare Noncompliance
- Value Conflicts

SUGGESTIONS FOR PROCESSING THIS EXERCISE WITH CLIENT

1. How did your feelings or views change when you did this exercise, especially from how you felt after completing the exercise on Step One?
2. Does this part of working a Twelve-Step program call on you to change your views about spiritual issues? If it does, what changes would you have to make?
3. Have you had experiences that seem to be signs of God or a Higher Power working in your life? What happened?
4. How does it feel to think about a Higher Power helping you overcome this problem?

STEP TWO: FINDING HOPE

> *This assignment is designed to help you work your Second Step. If you have already worked Step Two, please use this workbook to record the work you did then. When you've filled out this workbook, go through it with your Twelve-Step sponsor and your therapist.*

Do I Need to Be Restored to Sanity?

It was difficult enough to accept that we were powerless in Step One. Now this next Step is asking us to admit we're crazy, too! Think about it—how could anything *restore* us to sanity unless we had lost our sanity to start with? And yet, this can be a great source of hope.

With Step One and the realization that we were powerless over things that could kill us or ruin our lives, we faced a terrible situation. Most of us already knew inside that we were out of control—*"that our lives had become unmanageable"*—and this may have caused us a lot of depression and anxiety. If we had to stay stuck at that point, the future would be very dark.

However, with Step Two, we can find new hope. It says that being powerless doesn't mean our lives have to stay out of control, that we may find happiness and peace through "a Power greater than ourselves" taking control. That's why many people call this the Hope Step.

1. Do you feel your life has been insane? Why or why not? What does sanity mean to you?

    _____

    _____

    _____

2. What do you think of the idea of a Higher Power?

    _____

    _____

3. What experiences have you had that have led you to this view of a Higher Power?

    _____

    _____

    _____

236

4. How have you tried to make your life more sane than it was? How did your efforts work?

_____

_____

5. If your life has been out of control, and you've tried to straighten it out but couldn't, can you believe that a Power greater than you could do this? Would you want this to happen?

_____

_____

6. Here are some alternatives to the idea that a Higher Power could restore us to sanity. If one of these fits your beliefs better, please circle that letter.

   a. My life is not insane at all; I am in control and things are the way I want them to be.

   b. My life is insane but I can straighten things out myself.

   c. My life is insane but there is nothing either I or any Higher Power can do about it.

7. What would you have to gain, and to lose, by accepting the idea of a Higher Power that could create the order in your life that you may have wanted but been unable to produce?

   Gain   *Lose*

   _____   _____

   _____   _____

   _____   _____

   _____   _____

   _____   _____

8. Are the things in the Gain column worth the risk of losing the things in the Lose column?

   _____

9. If you are unable to believe in the idea of a Higher Power that can make your life better, do you wish you could believe in it? How would it change things if there were such a Higher Power?

   _____

   _____

10. Think of your sponsor, or other people from your Twelve-Step program that you like and respect. Have you talked about the Higher Power with these people? What were their views?

_____

_____

11. Have you heard a different explanation of God or a Higher Power that made sense to you? In general, what did it say?

_____

_____

12. Think about a Higher Power or God that would be good and would make sense to you, but would fit this world where bad things happen to good people. If you can imagine such a Higher Power or God, what would that Power be like?

_____

_____

13. If you have trouble believing in God, would it make a difference if you experienced an event or a feeling of having God or a Higher Power present? If you imagined a good version of God that would make sense to you, how would that God affect people's lives?

_____

_____

14. If such a Higher Power existed, how would you personally be able to tell? How would you see evidence of that God's actions? Would there be things to notice? What would they be?

_____

_____

15. How would your life be affected if there were a Higher Power doing the kinds of things in people's lives that the Twelve-Step programs describe?

_____

_____

16. What would have to happen—what would you have to see—for you to believe there was a Higher Power trying to help you?

   _____

   _____

17. Look back over your life, and think about whether you have had experiences where a Higher Power may have been helping you. What happened, and how have you explained it to yourself?

   _____

   _____

   _____

18. If you find yourself unable to definitely believe in the idea of a Higher Power, can you think of it as an unanswered question, with an open mind? What does it feel like to admit that it is at least possible? Does this cause you to feel any hope, or fear, or both?

   _____

   _____

Remember to bring completed work sheet to your next appointment.

Step Three:
Deciding to Turn It Over

GOALS OF THE EXERCISE

1. To assist the client in continuing to work the Twelve Steps.
2. To address the client's resistance to the idea of turning his or her will and life over to the care of God.
3. To increase the client's understanding of how people resolve spiritual issues in Twelve-Step programs.
4. To continue addressing spiritual issues that may interfere with success in recovery.

TYPES OF PROBLEMS THIS EXERCISE MAY BE MOST USEFUL FOR

- Adult Children of Alcoholic (ACOA) Traits
- Anger Management
- Antisocial Behavior
- Anxiety
- Blaming/Projection/Failure to Take Appropriate Responsibility
- Codependency
- Denial/Rationalization/Minimization of Substance-Abusing Behavior and/or Relapse Risk
- Depression
- Emotional Isolation
- Family Conflict
- General Interpersonal Relational Problems
- Generalized Treatment Resistance
- Grandiosity
- Hopelessness
- Impulsivity
- Inadequate Support Network
- Issues of Identity

- Learned Helplessness
- Low Self-Esteem
- Narcissistic Traits
- Peer Group Negativity
- Poor Social Skills
- Post-acute Withdrawal
- Resistance Based on Distorted Beliefs about Support Groups
- Shame Issues
- Spiritual Confusion
- Substance Abuse
- Substance Dependence
- Substance Withdrawal
- Tendency to Repeated Relapse
- Value Conflicts

SUGGESTIONS FOR PROCESSING THIS EXERCISE WITH CLIENT

1. How did your feelings or views change when you did this exercise?
2. Does this part of working a Twelve-Step program call on you to change your views and actions in regard to God and spiritual issues? If it does, what changes would you have to make?
3. Have you had experiences with acting on the guidance of a Higher Power? If you have, what happened?
4. How does it feel to think about seeking guidance from a Higher Power to overcome this problem?

STEP THREE: DECIDING TO TURN IT OVER

> *This assignment is designed to help you work your Third Step. Whether or not you have worked Step Three before, it would be a good idea to go through this workbook with your Twelve-Step sponsor and your therapist.*

Commitment and Action

The first Step asked us to admit what we could see clearly, that our lives were out of control. The second Step asked us to accept the idea that some Power greater than ourselves could straighten out the craziness in our lives. No real action was called for either time. Now Step Three asks us to make a decision to turn our will and our lives over to God!

For most of us, this idea has no appeal. First of all, we are raised to believe we should be in control of our lives. The idea of turning over control to anyone or anything else sounds crazy, like letting go of the steering wheel in traffic. Second, many have had bad experiences with religion, or have turned to God in despair and pain and seen nothing change.

However, the Twelve-Step experiences of millions of people over the past 60 years seem to prove that a relationship with a Higher Power might be worthwhile. Many of those people are highly intelligent—not likely to be conned or brainwashed. And they started out with the same doubts and suspicions about God that we are talking about now. But for millions of people like us, this Step came to make sense; and the results show that it seems to work.

1. Are you comfortable with what this Step asks you to do? If you aren't, what is it that bothers you or that you feel you might have a hard time doing?

   _____

   _____

2. Most of us have done our best to solve our problems before this. We've given them our best thought and our hardest efforts, but our best often hasn't been enough. What benefits do you think you might see if there were a God or Higher Power greater than yourself that would help, and you were able to turn your problems over to this God or Higher Power?

   _____

   _____

3. Some people recommend breaking this Step down into phrases and examining them one by one. To start with, the first phrase is *"Made a decision."* What does making a decision mean to you? What feeling comes to you when you think about making decisions about your life?

_____

_____

_____

4. *"Made a decision"* has the sound of a shift from thinking to action, either right away or in the future. Are you ready to decide on strong action to change some things in your life? If you still feel a need to think about it for a while longer, you can do that. The Step doesn't say that once we make this decision we have to "turn our will and our lives over" today. It says we have *decided* we will do so. Does thinking of it this way change the way this Step sounds to you? If so, how?

_____

_____

5. Do you feel ready to decide you will do this, even if not today? If you're stuck at this point, talk with your sponsor or a friend who's already gone through this—find out how that person felt and what happened. Other than talking with a friend or your sponsor, what can you do to find out more about this Step and to get answers for any questions or difficulties you have with it?

_____

_____

6. The next phrase is *"to turn our will and our lives over."* Turning something over sounds to many people as if the item being turned over is being handled carefully. Does this phrase carry this meaning for you? Or does it make you think of someone dropping something important without being sure anyone will catch it and keep it safe?

_____

_____

7. Have you had painful experiences with entrusting others with things that were important to you, such as possessions, information, decisions, or even your safety or the safety of someone else, and then being let down? _____ Do you feel this has happened with God? _____ If you answered "yes" to either of these, what happened and how did you feel about it then?

_____

_____

8. A big part of trust is learning how much trust we can give people or things. If we trust them to do something they can't do, we will be disappointed and maybe hurt. Has some-one failed to do what you trusted him or her to do? Can you see now that it was too much for that person, that he or she just didn't have the ability or character to do it? What happened, and how do you feel about it now?

    _____

    _____

9. To go on thinking about that last question, part of not being let down by God must be having a realistic understanding of what God can do. That brings us to the last phrase in this Step: "to the care of God *as we understood Him.*" Those last four words are very important.

    This Step doesn't ask us to trust anyone else's version of God. It asks us to set aside whatever we have been taught about God and start over. It requires us to figure out for ourselves what kind of God or Higher Power makes sense to us. How can you figure out for yourself what God might really be like?

    _____

    _____

    _____

10. Here is one way that has worked for other people.

    a. Find a quiet place to sit and think. Think about the fact that God is often referred to as a father. This may make you uneasy if your father was someone you couldn't trust and feel safe with. But think about being a parent. If you have children, think about how you feel about them, and if you don't have kids, think about how you would want to treat them if you did. First think about what you can do for your children. List some things you can do for them.

        _____

        _____

        _____

    b. Now think about the limits of what you can do for your children. What are the things you'd like to do for them, but can't? Dangers you can't protect them from? List some of those.

        _____

        _____

        _____

11. Can you protect your children from all the results of their own actions? _____ As parents we can do our best to teach our children, to advise them and warn them, but sometimes they still do things we know will hurt them and others. (Often they may hurt us!) How does it feel to think about your children making mistakes and being hurt, or hurting someone else, in spite of your efforts to teach and warn them?

   _____

   _____

12. Many people believe in a God who really is like a parent, who gives his children much of what they need and can teach and advise them, but who can't make them listen or take away their free will. This God can't keep his children from doing things that hurt them or others. This God gives support and guidance and does his best to give comfort and healing after bad things happen, but can't prevent many bad things that do happen. How does this compare with your picture of yourself as a parent?

   _____

   _____

13. Now think about the experiences you have had in your life, and the world as you see it around you. Would a God like this make sense in this world, and still be able to help you with your recovery from being dependent on a drug? If there were such a God, how could you tell?

   _____

   _____

14. One way many people feel they could tell would be that, in the same way we give things to our children, God would give them things they needed. Think back on your life. Were there times when something happened at just the right time for you in a way that seems hard to believe? Times when your luck was better than anyone would expect? What happened?

   _____

   _____

15. Another piece of evidence to look for is the advice a good parent gives his or her children. To see whether God has given us advice and warnings, we would need to know how God might communicate with us. Many people say that there were times when they felt a kind of inner voice, a hunch or gut feeling or conscience, urging them not to do something and giving them an uneasy feeling about it. What experiences like that have you had?

   _____

   _____

16. When you ignored that inner voice or feeling, what were the results of your actions?

_____

_____

17. Do you think that inner voice could have been a way for God to communicate with you? If that makes sense to you, how do you feel about the idea?

_____

_____

18. Another way some people feel God reaches out to them is through other people. What experiences have you had of someone showing up at just the right time in your life and helping you or telling you something you needed to hear?

_____

_____

19. Do you think that could have been another way for God to communicate with you, and if so, how do you feel about that idea?

_____

_____

20. If this way of thinking about God makes sense for you, it still leaves the question of how we "turn our will and our lives over." Since this idea of God is of a being whose powers are mainly to provide support and guidance, what would turning it over mean, so that we wouldn't be hurt again by trusting God to do things he wouldn't be able to do?

_____

_____

_____

21. For people who find this way of thinking about God useful, turning it over means looking to God for support and guidance. Do you feel you could listen for the guidance of your inner voice or conscience and follow that guidance? How would your life be different if you based your choices and actions on that guidance rather than on your own will?

_____

_____

_____

22. If you feel this makes sense and you can do this, that is one way of doing Step Three. You can turn your will and your life over to God by seeking his guidance and support from

246

your inner voice and then trusting and following that guidance, and by watching for the support of God in the good other people bring to you in your daily life.

There's another side to that. Since you also play a role in others' lives, this would also mean that at times God has acted through you. Have you ever been the one who was there at just the right time for someone else? What happened? How did you help the other person?

_____

_____

23. How does it feel to think about the idea that to other people, your actions might have been evidence of God's work in their lives?

_____

_____

24. If this discussion about God as a parent has not been helpful, there are other ways to think about the nature of God that have been useful for a lot of people. Some people think of God in ways guided by many Native American religious beliefs. Others think of something like the Force in the *Star Wars* films. The important things to do are these:

a. Spend time thinking about it, and decide for yourself what kind of God could exist, based on the experiences and information you have, and could be helpful to you.

b. Decide how you could tell if that God did exist. What evidence would there be?

c. Look for evidence—look for events that are harder to explain any other way.

25. Would you want the benefits of a good relationship with a God you could trust to help you? If you would, what would you be willing to do to have that in your life?

_____

_____

26. Now do another exercise in imagination. Imagine a future in which you have found answers to your questions and troubled feelings about God. Imagine yourself living knowing you could count on the guidance and support of a Higher Power—you see yourself living with greater confidence and peace of mind and knowing you will never have to face a problem alone and unsupported again. How does that mental picture look different from your life as it is now?

_____

_____

_____

27. How does it make you feel to think about that kind of life?_____

_____

_____

28. What can you do to start moving toward that life?_____

_____

_____

If you still are just not ready for Step Three, go back and spend some more time thinking about Steps One and Two. If you aren't ready to turn your will and life over to God yet, don't quit. You can attend a Twelve-Step program and get other benefits—people who accept, like, and respect you; good feedback and advice; structure and routine; a safe social circle; moral and emotional support. However, to have your best chance of staying clean and sober, and of being happy and successful in other areas of life, you can't work the Twelve Steps without Step Three.

Remember to bring completed work sheet to your next appointment.

Steps Four and Five: Personal Inventory

GOALS OF THE EXERCISE

1. To provide the client with a structured format for working Steps Four and Five of a Twelve-Step program.
2. To stimulate self-examination regarding problems related to addictions.
3. To empower the client to externalize and solve problems by analyzing thinking errors and dysfunctional relationship patterns.

TYPES OF PROBLEMS THIS EXERCISE MAY BE MOST USEFUL FOR

- Adult Children of Alcoholic (ACOA) Traits
- Anger Management
- Antisocial Behavior
- Anxiety
- Blaming/Projection/Failure to Take Appropriate Responsibility
- Codependency
- Denial/Rationalization/Minimization of Substance-Abusing Behavior and/or Relapse Risk
- Depression
- Emotional Isolation
- Family Conflict
- General Interpersonal Relational Problems
- Generalized Treatment Resistance
- Grandiosity
- Hopelessness
- Impulsivity
- Inadequate Support Network
- Issues of Identity
- Learned Helplessness

- Low Self-Esteem
- Narcissistic Traits
- Occupational Problems
- Parent-Child Relational Problems
- Partner Relational Problems
- Peer Group Negativity
- Poor Social Skills
- Post-acute Withdrawal
- Resistance Based on Distorted Beliefs about Support Groups
- Shame Issues
- Spiritual Confusion
- Substance Abuse
- Substance Dependence
- Substance Withdrawal
- Tendency to Repeated Relapse
- Treatment/Aftercare Noncompliance
- Value Conflicts

SUGGESTIONS FOR PROCESSING THIS EXERCISE WITH CLIENT

1. Did your understanding of the problem change when you wrote your inventory? If so, how?
2. What did you learn about your past actions and why you acted as you did?
3. What was it like to share your inventory with another person?
4. How did the person who heard your inventory react? In general, what kinds of things did he or she say to you? What was it like for you to hear that?

STEPS FOUR AND FIVE: PERSONAL INVENTORY

These two Steps are presented here as a single process, because that is how most recovering people experience them, though they are separate Steps. The writing and sharing of a personal inventory is a frightening and humbling task for many recovering people, but most also report great benefits once they complete these Steps. They say they feel great peace of mind, a strong sense of connection to other people and their Higher Power, and a feeling of making real progress in their recovery. If you have done these Steps before, discuss what this was like with your Twelve-Step sponsor, your therapist, or someone else in recovery whom you trust.

Why Write a "Searching and Fearless Moral Inventory" and Share It with Another Person?

1. What benefits do you think this process might offer—how could this help a person recover from alcoholism, other chemical dependence, or other addictive behaviors?

   _____

   _____

2. If you are like most people, these Steps are probably tough for you to carry out. If they are hard for you, what makes them difficult? Why do you feel they are hard for most people?

   _____

   _____

3. Here are the most common reasons people list for these Steps being hard—circle any that are true for you.

   a. We fear that the people who hear our inventories will reject us.

   b. We fear we will realize we are even worse than we thought we were.

   c. We find remembering old wrongs to be painful, embarrassing, and depressing.

   d. We feel focusing on past problems won't help us get better or change our futures.

   e. When we think about our whole lives up to now, the task seems overwhelming and we don't know how to get started.

251

4. Looking at the Big Book and other Twelve-Step literature, we find that this Step doesn't have to be that hard or complicated. In this workbook we will use a simple format. The first thing to do is to list your resentments. To do this, take a separate piece of paper and divide it into four columns. In the first column, list the people, the institutions or organizations, and the principles or rules that cause you to feel resentment. Focus on those that cause you to feel resentment now, and write them in the first column—finish the first column before going on to the second.

5. Now, in the second column, for each of the people, institutions, or principles you put in the first column, list what they have done to you, or what they might do, to cause your resentment. Again, fill this column out completely before moving on to the next one.

6. We tend to resent anything that we think might deprive us of something we want or need. In the third column, list the want or need in your life that these people, institutions, or principles have negatively affected. Choose from the following list:

   a. Self-esteem

   b. Relationships with other people

   c. Emotional security

   d. Physical and material security

   e. Sex

7. Twelve-Step writings also tell us that we are usually at least partly at fault in situations where we have resentments, and that our wrongs fall into four categories. In the fourth column, for each of these people, institutions, or principles, list anything you have done that has been motivated by one of the following.

   a. Selfishness

   b. Dishonesty

   c. Fear

   d. Inconsideration

8. This is your inventory related to resentments. Now do the same with fears; make the same kind of list of people, institutions, or principles that cause you to feel fear or anxiety, using the same four columns.

9. When you complete your inventory related to fears, you may find that it has most of the same names on it as the resentment inventory.

10. The final part of this "searching and fearless moral inventory" relates to our sexual behavior. Most alcoholics, addicts, and other compulsive people have had problems with this area of life. For this last part, take separate paper and list sexual wrongs. In the first column, again list people, institutions, or principles you have wronged. In the second column list what you did that was wrong. In column three, list what motivated your actions in each case, again choosing from:

   a. Self-esteem

   b. Relationships with other people

   c. Emotional security

   d. Physical and material security

   e. Sex

   Finally, in the fourth column list the category your wrong actions fit into, again choosing from:

   a. Selfishness

   b. Dishonesty

   c. Fear

   d. Inconsideration

11. Once you have completed these three sections, you have done your Step Four inventory. Of course, if there is other information you feel is important to include, write it down as well. But don't fall into the trap of working endlessly on your inventory and never finishing it. Do the best you can for now. You will find other things coming to mind in the future, and that's okay. Most recovering people do this over every now and then as they grow in understanding.

    However, we caution you not to deliberately leave your inventory incomplete. If there are things that you are afraid to write down, secrets you are afraid to share with anyone but that are interfering with your peace of mind, those are the most important things to list.

12. The Fifth Step is frightening for most of us. If you are worried by the idea of writing an inventory and sharing it with someone else, what are you afraid will happen?

_____

_____

_____

13. The two greatest fears most people feel are as follows: We fear that the people who hear our inventories will reject us—that we will lose their respect and friendship—and we fear that they will tell our secrets to others. Both of these fears are reasonable, and to keep these things from happening, it is important to choose the right kind of person to hear the inventory.

    Some people you might be able to trust with this could include your sponsor or another person from a Twelve-Step program, a close friend, a doctor or therapist, a priest or minister, or a trusted relative. Choose very carefully. Who might you choose to hear your own inventory?

    _____

    _____

14. Once you have chosen the person, talk to him or her and explain what you are doing, and what you are asking of him or her. If the person seems understanding and agrees to help you by hearing your inventory, choose a time and place where the two of you will have privacy and enough time to read through the inventory and talk about it. Then go and share this inventory with that person.

15. If your experience is like that of most people, the person hearing your inventory will not only continue to accept and respect you, he or she will share some of the problems you felt the most fear and shame about revealing. Once you have completed the Fifth Step, take a few minutes to sit quietly and notice how your feelings have changed. Most people find that they feel a huge sense of relief and a new peace of mind, as if a great burden has been lifted from them. They say they feel less isolated and more connected with others, and many even say they feel a strong sense of the presence of their Higher Power, some of them for the first time. Please list some of the feelings or thoughts that come to you.

    _____

    _____

    _____

    _____

16. Once you have completed Steps Four and Five, you are ready to move on to Steps Six and Seven, and it's best to do so as soon as you can. We will address these in the next assignment.

Remember to bring completed work sheet to your next appointment.

Steps Six and Seven:
Spiritual and Emotional Change

GOALS OF THE EXERCISE

1. To provide the client with a structured format for working Steps Six and Seven of a Twelve-Step program.
2. To stimulate openness to growth and positive change.
3. To empower the client to make positive changes in his or her self-image and interactions with others, replacing the dysfunctional patterns identified in Steps Four and Five with healthy alternatives.

TYPES OF PROBLEMS THIS EXERCISE MAY BE MOST USEFUL FOR

- Adult Children of Alcoholic (ACOA) Traits
- Anger Management
- Antisocial Behavior
- Anxiety
- Blaming/Projection/Failure to Take Appropriate Responsibility
- Codependency
- Denial/Rationalization/Minimization of Substance-Abusing Behavior and/or Relapse Risk
- Depression
- Emotional Isolation
- Family Conflict
- General Interpersonal Relational Problems
- Generalized Treatment Resistance
- Grandiosity
- Hopelessness
- Impulsivity
- Inadequate Support Network
- Issues of Identity

- Learned Helplessness
- Low Self-Esteem
- Narcissistic Traits
- Peer Group Negativity
- Poor Social Skills
- Post-acute Withdrawal
- Resistance Based on Distorted Beliefs about Substance Abuse/Dependence
- Resistance Based on Distorted Beliefs about Support Groups
- Shame Issues
- Spiritual Confusion
- Substance Abuse
- Substance Dependence
- Substance Withdrawal
- Tendency to Repeated Relapse
- Treatment/Aftercare Noncompliance
- Value Conflicts

SUGGESTIONS FOR PROCESSING THIS EXERCISE WITH CLIENT

1. Did you feel differently about any of your problems when you became willing to give them up?
2. How did your self-image and sense of your identity change with these steps?
3. What was it like to open yourself to being changed by a Higher Power?
4. How do you feel you have changed as a result of these steps?

STEPS SIX AND SEVEN: SPIRITUAL AND EMOTIONAL CHANGE

Like the last two Steps, Steps Six and Seven are presented as a single process. This phase of Twelve-Step recovery is linked to Step Three; in a way, this is where we carry out the decision we made in that Step to "turn our will and our lives over to the care of God as we understood Him." If you have done these Steps before, discuss what this was like with your Twelve-Step sponsor, your therapist, or someone else in recovery whom you trust.

Inviting Change

1. Let's start with Step Six. This Step asks us to be "entirely ready" to have God remove our defects of character. Keeping in mind the inventory you just wrote in Step Four, what does the phrase *defects of character* mean to you?

    _____

    _____

2. Looking at the things you listed in your inventory, think about what defects of character you feel led to these actions and situations in your life. You will probably see the same underlying patterns of thinking and feeling connected to all the things you listed in your inventory. What are these defects of character in your life?

    _____

    _____

    _____

3. We often find we feel the need to keep some defects of character because we don't see how we could get along and take care of ourselves without them. What are some of these patterns that you feel you have depended on to cope with life?

    _____

    _____

    _____

4. Have you tried to change these patterns before through willpower or intelligence? If you have, how well did that work? _____

5. This Step involves giving up the effort to control and make things happen ourselves, and trusting our Higher Power that we will be better and will like ourselves better after being changed by the removal of these problems. How do you feel about this trust?

_____

_____

6. How would your life be different if these defects of character were removed from you? What would you replace them with?

_____

_____

_____

7. Once you have become willing to be changed, does it make sense to you to ask your Higher Power to make this change? What does it feel like to do this instead of trying to do all the work yourself?

_____

8. Some people notice an immediate feeling of being different when they work Step Seven, such as the instant vanishing of their urges to drink or use. Others say they go through a more gradual change, not noticing a difference right away but seeing it over days, weeks, or months. Often others notice before we do that we have changed in small ways, such as finding ourselves being more considerate of other drivers in traffic, laughing about situations that used to cause us to feel anger or anxiety, being more patient with our children, and so on. What are changes you would like others to see in your daily actions and feelings as a result of these Steps?

_____

_____

_____

_____

Remember to bring completed work sheet to your next appointment.

Steps Eight and Nine: Making Amends

GOALS OF THE EXERCISE

1. To provide the client with a structured format for working Steps Eight and Nine of a Twelve-Step program.
2. To reduce anxiety and stress caused by unresolved interpersonal issues.
3. To eliminate shame and self-blame stemming from guilt over past abusive behavior toward others.
4. To enhance self-respect and empower the client by providing experiences of self-directed positive changes in interpersonal behavior patterns.

TYPES OF PROBLEMS THIS EXERCISE MAY BE MOST USEFUL FOR

- Adult Children of Alcoholic (ACOA) Traits
- Anger Management
- Antisocial Behavior
- Anxiety
- Blaming/Projection/Failure to Take Appropriate Responsibility
- Codependency
- Denial/Rationalization/Minimization of Substance-Abusing Behavior and/or Relapse Risk
- Depression
- Emotional Isolation
- Family Conflict
- General Interpersonal Relational Problems
- Generalized Treatment Resistance
- Grandiosity
- Impulsivity
- Inadequate Support Network
- Issues of Identity

- Legal Problems
- Low Self-Esteem
- Narcissistic Traits
- Occupational Problems
- Parent-Child Relational Problems
- Partner Relational Problems
- Peer Group Negativity
- Poor Social Skills
- Post-acute Withdrawal
- Resistance Based on Distorted Beliefs about Substance Abuse/Dependence
- Resistance Based on Distorted Beliefs about Support Groups
- Shame Issues
- Spiritual Confusion
- Substance Abuse
- Substance Dependence
- Substance Withdrawal
- Tendency to Repeated Relapse
- Treatment/Aftercare Noncompliance
- Value Conflicts

SUGGESTIONS FOR PROCESSING THIS EXERCISE WITH CLIENT

1. Did you feel anxiety about making amends to anyone? What were you afraid might happen?
2. How did your self-image and sense of identity change with these steps?
3. What was it like to face people you had hurt and acknowledge what you had done to them?
4. How did the people to whom you made amends react to this action on your part?
5. How did you feel when you completed your amends to each person on your list?
6. How do you feel your situation has changed as a result of these steps?
7. Are there people to whom you can't make amends? Why is this, and how will you handle those situations?

STEPS EIGHT AND NINE: MAKING AMENDS

Once again, we are combining two Steps in one worksheet, because they go together in the actions we take to carry them out. It is after these two Steps that A.A.'s Big Book tells us that the changes often referred to as the Promises will happen in our lives, and it is after these Steps that we reach the Maintenance Steps, as Steps Ten, Eleven, and Twelve are often called. Steps Eight and Nine are the ones that make the changes we are going though clearest to the people in our lives who have been affected by our addictive behaviors. They are also the most complicated Steps for most people and may raise some difficult questions. As with the previous Steps, if you have already done these, use this work sheet to record your actions, and talk this over with your therapist and your sponsor.

Why Stir up Old Problems by Making Amends?

1. This is another situation, like Steps Four and Five, where a difficult process is made easier by splitting it into two steps. We'll go even further, as we did with previous steps, and break each step down into phrases.

    The first thing Step Eight asks us to do is to make "a list of all persons we had harmed," in other words to identify who we've hurt, and what we've done to hurt them.

    Most people find that the lists of people and institutions they resented and feared, which they created in Step Four, make a good starting point for Step Eight. So let's start there. Please look again at those lists. On a separate sheet divided into three columns, list any of those people and institutions you have harmed in the first column. In the second column, list what you did in each case. Leave the third column blank for the time being.

2. Now think about how you feel about those people and institutions, and how they may feel about you. If you notice any of the same feelings showing up again and again in a lot of cases, on your part or the part of those you've hurt, list those feelings here.

    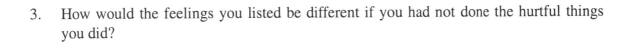

    _____

3. How would the feelings you listed be different if you had not done the hurtful things you did?

    _____

261

4. Have you experienced any situations where someone else hurt you, then tried to make amends to you? _____ How did you feel about that hurt, and then about those amends?

_____

_____

_____

5. What benefits do you think you would gain from making amends to the people and institutions you have listed? How do you think this will help you stay clean and sober, or avoid returning to any other addictive patterns?

_____

_____

_____

6. The next phrase is "and became willing to make amends to them all." Are you willing to do this, or do you find that in some of the situations you have listed, you are unwilling to make these amends? If so, why?

_____

_____

_____

7. Most of us find that we would rather not make at least some amends. The word *willing* is the key. It doesn't say we have to want to, or that we have to like doing so, only that we must be willing to do it. Give some examples of things you might be willing to do because they are needed, even though you'd prefer not to. _____

_____

8. Why are you willing to do these unpleasant things? Why are they necessary?

_____

_____

9. You may have said you are willing to do unpleasant things because the results of not doing them would be even more unpleasant. It's the same with these amends. What do you think you have to lose? In what ways might making these amends cause problems for you?

_____

_____

_____

10. Now balance the things you feel you might lose by making amends against the things you will lose if you relapse. Which set of consequences is worse, and why?

_____

11. If you have trouble understanding how failure to make amends might lead to relapse, think about how having these things unresolved affects your self-esteem and your level of anxiety. Talk about this with your sponsor or others you trust, and hint about how this interferes with your becoming the person you want to be, with the changes you asked your Higher Power to make in you in Step Seven. How would leaving amends unmade affect you in these areas?

_____

_____

12. If you've come to be willing to make all your amends, it's time to move on to Step Nine. Again, we'll break it down into phrases. The first part says we should make "direct amends to such people wherever possible." Turn to the third column on your list, and for each person or institution put down the action on your part that you feel is needed to make amends for your past actions. Remember the word _direct_. This means that if we have a choice between doing this face to face or by writing a letter, we do it face to face. It may be more uncomfortable this way, but the benefits are greater.

13. You may find that some of these amends are impossible to make. Some people on your list may be dead. Some may have moved away, and you might not know how to find them. You might not even know who some of them are. If this is the case, would you be willing to make these amends if you could? _____ The key is willingness. You may have to wait for the chance to make some amends for many years, but if you are ready to do so at the first opportunity, you can make this Step work for you.

14. You may also find that even if you can't make amends to a specific person or institution, you can change the way you treat people or institutions in general, and make amends that way. For example, a man who had been homeless in his addiction and had often spent his days lying on the lawn outside a library, frightening away some members of the community, made his amends by donating copies of recovery literature to that same library in his sobriety.

15. Before taking any action, we need to consider the second part of Step Nine: "except when to do so would injure them or others." What are some ways in which people could actually be further injured by someone making amends?

_____

_____

_____

16. Some answers to the last question would include situations where a person didn't know about the wrong we'd done, such as spouses who didn't know we'd been unfaithful. Other people might also be hurt, either because of the consequences to ourselves of our amends or in other ways. Looking again at your list of amends, are there some amends that would injure someone if you carried them out as you have written them down? If there are, what are they?

    _____

    _____

    _____

17. Are there other ways you can make any of those amends without harming anyone? How?

    _____

    _____

18. Once you've made your list of all the amends you need to make and can make without hurting anyone, talk it over with your sponsor or therapist or someone else whose judgment you trust, and get his or her ideas. Also, it's wise to get his or her advice about how you should approach these people. Here are some guidelines.

    a. Stick to talking about what you have done, not what they may have done to you. Remember, you're cleaning up your act, not theirs.

    b. You don't need to let yourself be victimized in this process. That's not healthy either.

    c. Keep in mind that you're doing this for your own recovery, and how they react is less important than how you feel afterward. Some people may be rude or ungrateful. As long as you're not doing this in a way that causes hurt, that's okay.

    Once you've made your list, eliminated anything that would hurt others (finding a different way to make the amends whenever you can), and gotten the feedback of someone you trust, it's time to get started. Go ahead and start contacting the people on your list, tell them why you want to speak with them, and carry out your amends. When you've made as many as you can, come back and answer the last question.

19. How do you feel now that you've made whatever amends you can for the time being? Do you feel that this will help you with your recovery from addiction? How does this help?

    _____

    _____

    _____

Remember to bring completed work sheet to your next appointment.

Steps Ten through Twelve:
Continued Growth

GOALS OF THE EXERCISE

1. To provide the client with a structured format for working Steps Ten through Twelve of a Twelve-Step program.
2. To reduce the likelihood of relapse into addiction or addictive behaviors.
3. To maintain and continue psychological and emotional growth and recovery.
4. To generalize the use of new cognitive and emotional coping mechanisms into all areas of life.

TYPES OF PROBLEMS THIS EXERCISE MAY
BE MOST USEFUL FOR

- Adult Children of Alcoholic (ACOA) Traits
- Anger Management
- Anxiety
- Blaming/Projection/Failure to Take Appropriate Responsibility
- Codependency
- Denial/Rationalization/Minimization of Substance-Abusing Behavior and/or Relapse Risk
- Depression
- Emotional Isolation
- Family Conflict
- General Interpersonal Relational Problems
- Generalized Treatment Resistance
- Grandiosity
- Hopelessness
- Impulsivity
- Inadequate Support Network
- Issues of Identity
- Learned Helplessness

- Low Self-Esteem
- Narcissistic Traits
- Occupational Problems
- Parent-Child Relational Problems
- Partner Relational Problems
- Peer Group Negativity
- Poor Social Skills
- Post-acute Withdrawal
- Resistance Based on Distorted Beliefs about Substance Abuse/Dependence
- Resistance Based on Distorted Beliefs about Support Groups
- Shame Issues
- Spiritual Confusion
- Substance Abuse
- Substance Dependence
- Substance Withdrawal
- Tendency to Repeated Relapse
- Treatment/Aftercare Noncompliance
- Value Conflicts

SUGGESTIONS FOR PROCESSING THIS EXERCISE WITH CLIENT

1. What ongoing changes do you see continuing in your life? What changes do you want to see?
2. How are other people reacting to these changes in you?
3. What situations do you think might make it tempting to relapse, and how can you use what you've learned to avoid relapse?
4. What specific actions are you including in your routine to continue working these Steps?

STEPS TEN THROUGH TWELVE: CONTINUED GROWTH

This time we're combining the last three Steps in one handout, again because they go together. These Steps are often called the Maintenance Steps, but continued growth *is a better term. Steps Ten through Twelve are the ones that help us avoid backsliding into old habits and thinking.*

Why Do I Need to Keep Doing This?

1. Unlike the first nine Steps, which we can start, carry out, and finish, these last three describe an ongoing process. What are some reasons for making this a never-finished program of action?

   _____

   _____

   _____

2. The first part of Step Ten says we should continue to take personal inventory. How do you do this in your own life?

   _____

   _____

3. The next phrase is "and when we were wrong promptly admitted it." Why should we do this? How will it help us?

   _____

   _____

4. Continuing to Step Eleven, we are asked to seek through prayer and meditation to improve our conscious contact with God as we understand him. How can you do this?

   _____

   _____

5. If you're uncomfortable with prayer and meditation, or feel you don't know how to do them, who can you ask for guidance on this?

_____

_____

6. What does "conscious contact with God as we understood Him" mean to you?

_____

_____

_____

7. If you recall some of the questions you answered about Step Three, they talked about different ways God might be communicating with us. What ideas did you find worked best for you, and can you see ways this communication could be made clearer?

_____

_____

_____

8. How would having clearer communication with the God or Higher Power of your understanding help you?

_____

_____

_____

9. How can you use prayer or meditation to improve your ability to be aware of and understand this communication or "conscious contact"?

_____

_____

10. How are you doing this in your daily life?

_____

_____

11. The second part of Step Eleven says we are praying only for knowledge of God's will for us and the power to carry that out. Why do you think this is written this way, instead of telling us to figure out ourselves what's best for us and pray for that to happen?

_____

_____

12. When you were drinking, using, or engaged in other addictive behaviors, did you make mistakes about what was best for you and what needed to happen in your life? _____ Are you immune from that type of mistaken thinking now, or do you still catch yourself making mistakes in this area? If you still make mistakes like this, please give an example.

_____

_____

13. How can you become more aware of what your God or Higher Power is trying to guide you toward in your life? Do you think that inner voice, gut feeling, or conscience we discussed earlier could be a good guide? _____ How could you try to be sure you were really following the guidance of your Higher Power instead of your own addictive thinking patterns? Do you think talking with others about your thoughts would help? _____ If you do, who would be the best people to talk with about this?

_____

14. The last part of Step Eleven asks for "the power to carry that out." How could your God or Higher Power help in this area?

_____

_____

_____

15. Step Twelve starts out, "Having had a spiritual awakening as the result of these Steps . . ." Do you feel you've had a spiritual awakening? _____ What does this phrase mean to you?

_____

16. Some people say that "a spiritual awakening" is a fancy way to say "a change of attitude." Have you had a change of attitude? _____ If so, how would you describe this change?

_____

17. Do you feel that your spiritual awakening or change of attitude is "the result of these Steps"? If so, how have the Steps changed you?

_____

_____

_____

18. The next part of Step Twelve says that we are to try to "carry this message to others," either alcoholics if we are involved in A.A., or addicts if our program is N.A., or others with other programs—whoever has the same problems we have overcome. How can you do this, and how much are you doing so now?

_____

_____

_____

19. What benefits do you get from doing this—how does it help you in your recovery?

_____

_____

20. The final part of Step Twelve says that we "practice these principles in all our affairs." What does this mean to you?

_____

_____

_____

21. How are you carrying out this part of Step Twelve in your own daily life?

_____

_____

_____

_____

22. What benefits do you get from practicing these principles in all your affairs? Why should you do this, and how does it help you in your recovery?

_____

_____

_____

At this point you have worked your way through all the Twelve Steps and, if you are continuing to practice Steps Ten through Twelve, are using a system that has helped many millions of people avoid relapse and continue to grow in peace of mind and ability to handle life's difficulties. If you are actively practicing your program, you have a support group of people who know you, accept you, and care what happens to you. You are also a support to others, and are growing in ability to be the person you wish to be.

To conclude this series of work sheets, we will review the Promises that Twelve-Step literature tells us we can expect to come true for us if we continue to work at this. From the Big Book (Alcoholics Anonymous World Services, Inc., 1976, p. 83–84):

"If we are painstaking about this phase of our development, we will be amazed before we are halfway through. We are going to know a new freedom and a new happiness. We will not regret the past nor wish to shut the door on it. We will comprehend the word serenity and we will know peace. No matter how far down the scale we have gone, we will see how our experience can benefit others. That feeling of uselessness and self-pity will disappear. We will lose interest in selfish things and gain interest in our fellows. Self-seeking will slip away. Our whole attitude and outlook upon life will change. Fear of people and of economic insecurity will leave us. We will intuitively know how to handle situations which used to baffle us. We will suddenly realize that God is doing for us what we could not do for ourselves."

Remember to bring completed work sheet to your next appointment.

Finding and Working with a Twelve-Step Sponsor

GOALS OF THE EXERCISE

1. To provide the client with a rationale and methods for finding and working with a Twelve-Step program sponsor.
2. To strengthen the client's interpersonal support network and reduce social isolation.
3. To enhance the client's Twelve-Step work and reduce his or her likelihood of relapse into addiction or addictive behaviors.
4. To accelerate the client's acquisition of improved thinking and coping skills by exposure to those used successfully by others on the client's issues.

TYPES OF PROBLEMS THIS EXERCISE MAY BE MOST USEFUL FOR

- Adult Children of Alcoholic (ACOA) Traits
- Anger Management
- Anxiety
- Blaming/Projection/Failure to Take Appropriate Responsibility
- Codependency
- Denial/Rationalization/Minimization of Substance-Abusing Behavior and/or Relapse Risk
- Depression
- Emotional Isolation
- Family Conflict
- General Interpersonal Relational Problems
- Generalized Treatment Resistance
- Grandiosity
- Hopelessness
- Impulsivity
- Issues of Identity
- Low Self-Esteem

- Narcissistic Traits
- Occupational Problems
- Parent-Child Relational Problems
- Partner Relational Problems
- Poor Social Skills
- Post-acute Withdrawal
- Resistance Based on Distorted Beliefs about Substance Abuse/Dependence
- Resistance Based on Distorted Beliefs about Support Groups
- Shame Issues
- Spiritual Confusion
- Substance Abuse
- Substance Dependence
- Substance Withdrawal
- Tendency to Repeated Relapse
- Treatment/Aftercare Noncompliance
- Value Conflicts

SUGGESTIONS FOR PROCESSING THIS EXERCISE WITH CLIENT

1. What people did you consider asking to be your sponsor? What qualities about them made you feel they would be helpful?
2. How do you include contact with your sponsor in your regular routine?
3. How is your relationship with your sponsor helping you?
4. What could you do to gain more benefit from working with your sponsor?
5. Are there areas where your sponsor has not been helpful, and if so, what are they? Have you talked about this with him or her, and if so, what was the outcome?

FINDING AND WORKING WITH A TWELVE-STEP SPONSOR

One of the first things most people hear when they attend Twelve-Step meetings is a lot of talk about sponsors, and probably frequent advice to find one. This work sheet will help you in that process. It is a good idea to talk over everything on this sheet, plus any other questions or ideas you have, with your therapist.

Why Do I Need a Sponsor?

1. To start out, please describe your general impression of what a sponsor is and what he or she would do for you.

   _____

   _____

2. Some other words people use to describe a sponsor might include these: *teacher, coach, tutor, mentor, guide.* Do these words give you a different mental picture than the first one you had when you heard people talking about sponsors? If so, how are the two pictures different?

   _____

   _____

3. Have you learned skills in the past with the help of a teacher, coach, or tutor? How were these people able to help you?

   _____

   _____

4. If you're like most people, you find that the qualities that make others most helpful to us in learning new skills include the following:

   • They are respectful to us.
   • They understand us.
   • They use terms we can understand.
   • They know what they're talking about.
   • They are encouraging.
   • They find a balance between pushing us and being patient with us.

Now think of the people you've learned from in the past, the ones who were the biggest help to you. Which of the qualities just listed did they have?

_____

_____

_____

5. How would it be to have someone like this help you with your questions and problems in getting clean and sober?

_____

_____

6. How could you find a person like this to work with you?

_____

_____

_____

7. Do you have a problem with the idea of someone helping you learn the skills of clean and sober life? If so, what bothers you about this idea?

_____

_____

_____

8. How can you overcome these objections so that you are able to work with a sponsor—is there something a possible sponsor or your therapist could do to help you with this? If so, what is it?

_____

_____

9. Here are some recommendations many people experienced in recovery offer about working with a sponsor. They will often say that a sponsor should have the following characteristics:

    •   Someone who says things in meetings that you find help you with your own questions
    •   Someone you feel comfortable with and feel you could trust
    •   Someone who has his or her own sponsor and works with that sponsor regularly
    •   Someone who has worked the Steps him- or herself and has at least a year of clean and sober time

- Someone who seems to have a balanced life without a lot of crises in it
- Someone with whom there is no possibility of a sexual attraction developing to interfere with your recovery work—usually a person of the same gender as yourself
- Someone who is not already in a close family, work, or friendship relationship with you

During the next few meetings you attend, pick out some people who seem to fit this profile and list their names here.

_____

_____

_____

10. Of the people you have listed, who would be most helpful to you in learning to work a Twelve-Step program and handle life's issues without relapsing?

_____

_____

11. How will you approach this person and ask him or her to be your sponsor?

_____

_____

_____

12. When will you do this? Pick a time, talk it over with your therapist, and follow through.

_____

_____

13. To be answered after you find a sponsor: What was it like asking this person to be your sponsor—how did you feel, and what did you expect to happen?

_____

_____

14. When and where will you talk with your sponsor each week?

Remember to bring completed work sheet to your next appointment.

Finding a Home Group

GOALS OF THE EXERCISE

1. To provide the client with a rationale and method for finding and working with a Twelve-Step home group.
2. To strengthen the client's interpersonal support network and reduce social isolation.
3. To enhance the client's Twelve-Step work and reduce the likelihood of relapse into addiction or addictive behaviors.
4. To accelerate the client's acquisition of improved social and communication skills by frequent interaction with others in a healthy community setting.

TYPES OF PROBLEMS THIS EXERCISE MAY BE MOST USEFUL FOR

- Adult Children of Alcoholic (ACOA) Traits
- Anxiety
- Codependency
- Denial/Rationalization/Minimization of Substance-Abusing Behavior and/or Relapse Risk
- Depression
- Emotional Isolation
- General Interpersonal Relational Problems
- Generalized Treatment Resistance
- Grandiosity
- Inadequate Support Network
- Living Environment Deficiencies (Relapse Triggers, Lack of Emotional Support, etc.)
- Low Self-Esteem
- Narcissistic Traits
- Peer Group Negativity
- Poor Social Skills
- Post-acute Withdrawal

- Resistance Based on Distorted Beliefs about Substance Abuse/Dependence
- Resistance Based on Distorted Beliefs about Support Groups
- Shame Issues
- Spiritual Confusion
- Substance Abuse
- Substance Dependence
- Substance Withdrawal
- Tendency to Repeated Relapse
- Treatment/Aftercare Noncompliance

Suggestions for Processing This Exercise with Client

1. What does it feel like for you to belong to a supportive group of people?
2. What kinds of comments do the others in this group make to you about yourself? Do these comments match the way you feel about yourself? If not, why do you think these people see you differently than you see yourself?
3. How is your participation in this group helping you?
4. What could you do to gain more benefit from being a member of this group?
5. Do you have some problems or questions you feel no one in this group could understand or help you with? What are they? What do you think would happen if you brought them up in the group?

FINDING A HOME GROUP

> *One of the things we hear mentioned often in Twelve-Step meetings is having a home group, and possibly invitations to make a certain group one's home group. This worksheet will help you choose a home group and get the most out of belonging to it. It is a good idea to talk over everything on this sheet, plus any other questions or ideas you have, with your therapist.*

What's a Home Group For?

1. To start with, let's look at why people call a group a *home group*. When you hear the word *home* what thoughts come to your mind?

   _____

   _____

2. To most of us, *home* means any or all of these things:

   • A place where we are known and accepted
   • A place where we are safe and can relax
   • A place where we are loved
   • A place where we are missed if we aren't there
   • A place where we share important parts of our lives with others who care about us
   • A place where we are involved in important decisions that affect us and others

   How many of these are important to you? Please circle the ones you would like to have in your life. What are some other situations where you've found these things in your own life?

   _____

   _____

3. Some of the places many of us find those things include our families, churches, social clubs, athletic teams, or our workplaces. Do you find these situations give you the things we connected with the word *home,* or not?

   _____

   _____

   _____

4. Now think about people you have seen socializing with each other before or after (or during) Twelve-Step meetings you've attended. Did they seem to be finding some or all of the things we just listed in those meetings? Which things?

_____

_____

_____

5. Especially in situations where we have grown up in families where addiction or other problems caused serious difficulties, we may never have experienced the feelings we connected with *home* anywhere in our lives before. People in this situation tend to feel lonely and as if they don't fit in anywhere, and may try to find a replacement "family" to fill the needs their biological families couldn't. We often seek escape from these feelings in alcohol or other drugs. How often do you feel this way, and is there any place, group, or activity you have been using to escape loneliness? If so, how has it worked?

_____

_____

6. To explain the idea of a home group simply, it is a meeting that you have chosen to iden-tify yourself with, which you attend regularly. If you are a member of this group, you may find your sponsor there (see the handout entitled "Finding and Working with a Twelve-Step Sponsor"). You may take on some responsibilities for that group, such as getting to the meeting place early and making coffee, or cleaning up after meetings, or being the treasurer. You will probably participate in the group's discussion and decisions about issues affecting the whole group, usually referred to as a group conscience.

   Many people actually think of their home groups as a second family, one they have chosen, which meets their needs for family ties in ways their birth families may not be able to do. How do you think you would feel about the idea of belonging to a second family of this kind?

_____

_____

7. In your attendance at different meetings, you may have noticed that you feel most com-fortable in certain types of groups. What meetings or kinds of meetings make you feel most at home?

_____

_____

8. In the meetings you like, how have you noticed people treating each other like family members?

    _____

    _____

9. How could belonging to such a group help you cope with and solve problems in your life?

    _____

    _____

10. As part of your recovery program, your therapist may ask you to choose a home group. Whether this is the case or not, you will probably find it benefits you to do so. Please list at least one group that you would like to have as a home group. _____

11. What is it about this group that makes it more appealing to you than other groups?_____

    _____

    _____

12. When and where does this group meet, and how often will you attend? _____

    _____

    _____

Remember to bring completed work sheet to your next appointment.

Balancing My Twelve-Step Program, My Family Life, and My Work Life

GOALS OF THE EXERCISE

1. To reduce potential family tension and conflicts in early recovery.
2. To assist the client in avoiding work-related difficulties undermining his or her early sobriety.

TYPES OF PROBLEMS THIS EXERCISE MAY BE MOST USEFUL FOR

- Adult Children of Alcoholic (ACOA) Traits
- Blaming/Projection/Failure to Take Appropriate Responsibility
- Burnout
- Codependency
- Emotional Isolation
- Family Conflict
- Generalized Treatment Resistance
- Inadequate Support Network
- Issues of Identity
- Living Environment Deficiencies (Relapse Triggers, Lack of Emotional Support, etc.)
- Low Self-Esteem
- Occupational Problems
- Parent-Child Relational Problems
- Partner Relational Problems
- Peer Group Negativity
- Poor Social Skills
- Resistance Based on Distorted Beliefs about Substance Abuse/Dependence
- Resistance Based on Distorted Beliefs about Support Groups
- Shame Issues
- Substance Abuse

- Substance Dependence
- Tendency to Repeated Relapse
- Treatment/Aftercare Noncompliance
- Value Conflicts

SUGGESTIONS FOR PROCESSING THIS EXERCISE WITH CLIENT

1. How do members of your family feel about the amount of time you are putting into staying clean and sober?

2. What kinds of comments do members of your family make about your going to Twelve-Step meetings? Do they seem to understand and approve of what you are doing?

3. Have the attitudes of family members about your attending meetings changed since you began participating in a Twelve-Step program? How have they changed, and why do you think this has happened? If your family members object, what ways can you see to meet their objections and continue attending your meetings?

4. How much time do you put into Twelve-Step meetings and other activities each week? How much time do you spend with your family? How do these amounts compare?

5. Do you feel pressured to do more than you are doing at work? If you did do more, how would this affect your family life and your participation in your recovery program? If you didn't, what would the consequences in your workplace be?

BALANCING MY TWELVE-STEP PROGRAM, MY FAMILY LIFE, AND MY WORK LIFE

One of the most important parts of recovery is balance in our lives. Three of the most important parts of our lives at this stage are recovery activities, family life, and work life. We may find these in conflict, however, and by trying to do all we feel we should be doing in one area, we may neglect the others. So balance may be difficult to achieve. It is a good idea to talk over everything on this sheet, plus any other questions or ideas you have, with your therapist.

Why Is Balance So Hard to Achieve?

1. One of the key characteristics of an addictive lifestyle is a lack of balance; in other words, in anything we do, we either go overboard or don't do nearly enough. What are some ways in which you went overboard and did too much in your life before you began your recovery?

    _____

    _____

    _____

2. What are some aspects of your life that you neglected before recovery, doing too little?

    _____

    _____

    _____

3. We often go to extremes in recovery programs too, especially in our early sobriety. If you have seen this in your life, what tells you you're going to excess, and what are the consequences?

    _____

    _____

    _____

284

4. Since we may have neglected our families, we may tend to go overboard with them too. This may cause problems because they've gotten used to getting along without us being around much, and now we feel they're shutting us out. Has this happened in your life? What happened?

_____

_____

_____

5. On the other hand, our families may feel we continue to neglect them to spend time with our newfound friends and activities in recovery. There may be some truth to this, as some of us get so absorbed in rebuilding our lives at work and in our recovery programs that we still have trouble finding time for our families. Has this happened in your family? What happened?

_____

_____

_____

6. With work, too, it's easy for us to get carried away. We want to repair our damaged reputations, and we may also fall into workaholism, a pattern in which we lose ourselves in work the way we used to lose ourselves in drinking and using, as a way to numb ourselves. If this happens, we may find we feel the need to put so much into work that we resent the demands of both our families and our recovery programs. Have you seen signs of workaholism in your life? What has happened to make you suspect you are working too much?

_____

_____

7. Although it is very important to spend a lot of time and attention on our recovery, we can even put too much into this, if it leads to our neglecting responsibilities in other parts of life. This, in turn, can lead us to get burned out on recovery and quit working at it, then drift into a relapse. Have you seen examples of this in your own life or others? What were the consequences?

_____

_____

_____

8. One key to maintaining balance is getting accurate feedback from other people who know us. Our families are among those who know us best, but they may be too emo-

tionally involved to see clearly how we are doing. So we should give the comments of our family members careful attention; and the more they understand about what we are doing, the more helpful their ideas will be. What are some ways we can include our families in our recovery programs and help them better understand what we are doing?

_____

_____

_____

9. How much does your family seem to understand your addiction and your recovery program? What parts do they seem unable to understand?

_____

_____

_____

10. How could your family be more helpful to you if they understood more about what you are doing?

_____

_____

_____

11. We may see that our family members could benefit from joining a support group such as Al-Anon or Alateen; but they might feel that they have been doing a better job of dealing with life than we have for a long time, and resent our seeming to tell them what they need to do. Has this happened in your family? _____ Often, we find that our families stay angry or mistrustful of us for a long time after we begin our recovery, and they may be very skeptical or scornful about any aspect of that recovery including Twelve-Step groups. It is best to avoid being pushy or defensive, even if (especially if!) we think family members might benefit from attending such a group. What would be some ways you could handle this differently, hopefully without getting into an argument?

_____

_____

_____

12. Here are some ways many recovering people have helped family and friends understand how their recovery and their Twelve-Step programs worked, which you might be able to use.

a. Invite them to meetings with you.

b. Introduce them to friends from the program, especially your sponsor.

c. Take them to program social functions.

d. Offer them program literature.

e. Tell them about meetings.

f. Introduce them to family members of other members of the program.

Which of these seem most likely to be useful in helping your family understand your recovery?

_____

_____

13. If for a while family members don't seem to understand, believe, or appreciate the change in you, be patient. This can also be a good topic to bring up for discussion in your group, or to talk about with your sponsor, or to talk about in family therapy. List here some people who might be able to help you in helping your family and friends to understand your Twelve-Step program.

_____

_____

14. Regarding work, this may be easier than you think. Most alcoholics and addicts are excellent workers when they are clean and sober, and often find they expect more of themselves than anyone else would ask of them. Have you had experiences where you found you were judging your work performance more harshly than your supervisors? If so, what happened?

_____

_____

_____

15. The chances are your supervisor already knows about your problems with alcohol, other drugs, or compulsive behaviors, or at least knows you had some kind of serious problem affecting your work. If you explain what you are doing now to overcome this problem, your supervisor may be supportive and understanding, and you will probably find that you don't need to push yourself as hard as you think to regain your good standing on the job.

Every situation is different and it's wise to talk with your family, your sponsor, and your therapist first, but if you are finding that your work's demands are undermining your recovery or your family life, you will probably have to address this to avoid relapsing or causing further difficulties with your family.

Remember, even people who aren't newly recovering from addiction have trouble balancing work, family, and self-care in today's world. The fact that you're having difficulty with this doesn't mean you're doing it wrong, it just means you're human. Keep seeking out the views of others to avoid slipping back into distorted attitudes, excess, and overly harsh self-criticism.

This is a good topic to discuss in your group and with your family, your sponsor, and your therapist. List here some people who might be able to help you prepare for a talk with your supervisor about your recovery program and what you need to do to take care of yourself.

_____

_____

_____

Remember to bring completed work sheet to your next appointment.

Bibliography and Suggested Reading

Ackerman, R. J. (1983). *Children of alcoholics: A guide for parents, educators, and therapists* (2nd ed.). New York: Fireside.

Alcoholics Anonymous World Services, Inc. (1976). *Alcoholics Anonymous: The story of how many thousands of men and women have recovered from alcoholism* (3rd ed.). New York: Alcoholics Anonymous World Services.

Beck, A. T., Emery, G., Rush, A. J., & Shaw, B. F. (1979). *Cognitive therapy of depression.* New York: Guilford.

Bedell, J. R., & Lennox, S. S. (1997). *Handbook for communications and problem-solving skill training.* New York: Wiley.

Berg, I. K., & Miller, S. D. (1992). *Working with the problem drinker: A solution-focused approach.* New York: Norton.

Bernstein, N. (1996). *Treating the unmanageable adolescent.* Northvale, NJ: Aronson.

Birnes, B., & Mastrich, J. (1988). *The ACOA's guide to raising healthy children.* New York: Macmillan.

Center for Substance Abuse Treatment. (1994). *Treatment Improvement Protocol (TIP) Series 8: Intensive outpatient treatment for alcohol and other drug abuse.* Rockville, MD: U.S. Department of Health and Human Services.

Center for Substance Abuse Treatment. (1994). *Treatment Improvement Protocol (TIP) Series 9: Assessment and treatment of patients with coexisting mental illness and alcohol and other drug abuse.* Rockville, MD: U.S. Department of Health and Human Services.

Center for Substance Abuse Treatment. (1997). *Treatment Improvement Protocol (TIP) Series 25: Substance abuse treatment and domestic violence.* Rockville, MD: U.S. Department of Health and Human Services.

Clancy, J. (1996). *Anger and addiction: Breaking the relapse cycle—A teaching guide for professionals.* Madison, CT: Psychosocial Press.

Co-Dependents Anonymous. (1995). *Co-Dependents Anonymous.* Phoenix, AZ: Co-Dependents Anonymous.

Cruse, J., Mende, C., Radcliffe, A., Rush, P., & Scott, C. F. (1993). *The pharmer's almanac II: an updated training manual on the pharmacology of psychoactive drugs.* Denver, CO: Mac Publishing.

Edwards, J. T. (1990). *Treating chemically dependent families.* Minneapolis, MN: Johnson Institute.

Eisenberg, A., Eisenberg, H., & Mooney, A. J. (1992). *The recovery book.* New York: Workman.

Emotions Anonymous International. (1978). *Emotions Anonymous.* Saint Paul, MN: Emotions Anonymous International.

Evans, K., & Sullivan, J. M. (1995). *Treating addicted survivors of trauma.* New York: Guilford.

Farmer, S. (1989). *Adult children of abusive parents: A healing program for those who have been physically, sexually, or emotionally abused.* New York: Ballantine.

Foy, D. W. (Ed.). (1992). *Treating PTSD: Cognitive-behavioral strategies.* New York: Guilford.

Gamblers Anonymous. (1984). *GA: Sharing recovery through Gamblers Anonymous.* Los Angeles: Gamblers Anonymous.

Gorski, T. T. (1989). *Understanding the Twelve Steps.* New York: Fireside.

Gorski, T. T., & Miller, M. (1986). *Staying sober: A guide for relapse prevention.* Independence, MO: Herald House.

Hayes, E. N. (Ed.). (1989). *Adult children of alcoholics remember: True stories of abuse and recovery by ACOAs.* New York: Harmony.

Heggenhougen, H. K. (1997). *Reaching new highs: Alternative therapies for drug addicts.* Northvale, NJ: Aronson.

Hesley, J. G., & Hesley, J. W. (1998). *Rent two films and let's talk in the morning: Using popular movies in psychotherapy.* New York: Wiley.

Lenz, B. S., & Finley, J. R. (1999). *The chemical dependence treatment documentation sourcebook.* New York: Wiley.

Malekoff, A. (1997). *Group work with adolescents.* New York: Guilford.

Matsakis, A. (1994). *Post-traumatic Stress Disorder: A complete treatment guide.* Oakland, CA: New Harbinger.

Matsakis, A. (1996). *I can't get over it: A handbook for trauma survivors* (2nd ed.). Oakland, CA: New Harbinger.

McFarlane, A. C., van der Kolk, B. A., & Weisaeth, L. (Eds.). (1996). *Traumatic stress: The effects of overwhelming experience on mind, body, and society.* New York: Guilford.

McMillin, C. S., & Rogers, R. L. (1989). *The healing bond: Treating addictions in groups.* New York: Norton.

Miller, W. R., & Rollnick, S. (1991). *Motivational interviewing: Preparing people to change addictive behavior.* New York: Guilford.

National Institute on Alcohol Abuse and Alcoholism. (1995). *Twelve Step facilitation therapy manual.* Rockville, MD: U.S. Department of Health and Human Services.

National Institute on Alcohol Abuse and Alcoholism. (1997). *Improving compliance with alcoholism treatment.* Rockville, MD: U.S. Department of Health and Human Services.

National Institute on Drug Abuse. (1993). *Diagnostic source book on drug abuse research and treatment.* Rockville, MD: U.S. Department of Health and Human Services.

National Institute on Drug Abuse. (1994). *Clinical report series: Mental health assessment and diagnosis of substance abusers.* Rockville, MD: U.S. Department of Health and Human Services.

Ortman, D. (1997). *The dually diagnosed: A therapist's guide to helping the substance abusing, psychologically disturbed patient.* Northvale, NJ: Aronson.

Overeaters Anonymous. (1980). *Overeaters Anonymous.* Rio Rancho, NM. Overeaters Anonymous.

Schaeffer, B. (1987). *Is it love or is it addiction?* Center City, MN: Hazelden.

Schultheis, G. M. (1998). *Brief therapy homework planner.* New York, NY: Wiley.

Sex and Love Addicts Anonymous. (1986). *Sex and Love Addicts Anonymous: The basic text for the Augustine Fellowship.* Boston, MA: The Augustine Fellowship, Sex and Love Addicts Anonymous.

Sherwood, V. R. (1998). *Getting past resistance in psychotherapy with the out-of-control adolescent.* Northvale, NJ: Aronson.

Trimpey, J. (1996). *Rational recovery: The new cure for substance addiction.* New York: Pocket Books.

Wiger, D. E. (1997). *The clinical documentation sourcebook.* New York: Wiley.

Woititz, J. G. (1983). *Adult children of alcoholics.* Pompano Beach, FL: Health Communications.

Woititz, J. G. (1992). *Healthy parenting: An empowering guide for adult children.* New York: Fireside.

Yalom, I. D. (1980). *Existential psychotherapy.* New York: Basic Books.

Yalom, I. D. (1995). *The theory and practice of group psychotherapy* (4th ed.). New York: Basic Books.

Z., Phillip. (1990). *A skeptic's guide to the 12 Steps.* Center City, MN: Hazelden.

Quick Cross-Reference Problem/Assignment Guide

Adult Children of Alcoholic (ACOA) Traits

Exercises I.2, I.4, II.2, II.3, III.2, III.4, III.5, IV.2, IV.3, IV.4, IV.5, IV.7, IV.8, IV.9, V.4, VI.4, VI.7, VII.2, VII.5, VII.6, VIII.1, VIII.2, VIII.3, VIII.4, VIII.5, VIII.6, VIII.7, VIII.8, VIII.9, VIII.11, VIII.12

Anger Management

Exercises I.3, I.4, II.3, II.4, II.5, III.3, III.5, IV.2, IV.3, IV.4, IV.6, V.3, VI.1, VI.2, VI.5, VI.6, VI.7, VII.2, VII.6, VIII.3, VIII.4, VIII.5, VIII.6, VIII.7, VIII.8, VIII.9, VIII.10

Antisocial Behavior

Exercises II.3, II.4, II.5, IV.1, IV.3, IV.4, IV.8, V.2, VI.2, VI.6, VI.7, VIII.5, VIII.6, VIII.8

Anxiety

Exercises I.3, III.1, III.2, III.3, III.4, III.5, IV.2, IV.3, IV.5, IV.6, IV.7, V.1, V.3, VI.1, VI.2, VI.4, VII.1, VII.2, VII.3, VII.5, VII.6, VIII.1, VIII.2, VIII.3, VIII.4, VIII.5, VIII.6, VIII.7, VIII.8, VIII.9, VIII.10, VIII.11

Appetite Disturbance

Exercises I.3, III.5, IV.5, V.3, VII.1, VII.2, VII.4

Blaming/Projection/Failure to Take Appropriate Responsibility

Exercises I.1, I.2, I.4, I.5, II.3, II.4, II.5, III.5, IV.8, V.4, VI.1, VI.2, VI.3, VI.5, VI.6, VI.7, VII.3, VII.5, VII.6, VIII.1, VIII.3, VIII.4, VIII.5, VIII.6, VIII.7, VIII.8, VIII.9, VIII.10, VIII.12

Borderline Traits

Exercises I.4, II.3, III.1, III.2, III.3, IV.2, IV.3, IV.4, IV.5, IV.7, IV.8, IV.9, V.2, VI.4, VI.5, VII.2, VII.5, VII.6

Burnout

Exercises I.3, III.3, IV.3, IV.5, VI.2, VII.5, VII.6, VIII.12

Codependency

Exercises I.3, I.4, II.3, III.2, III.3, III.4, III.5, IV.2, IV.3, IV.4, IV.5, IV.7, IV.8, IV.9, VI.2, VI.4, VII.5, VII.6, VIII.1, VIII.3, VIII.4, VIII.5, VIII.6, VIII.7, VIII.8, VIII.9, VIII.10

Denial/Rationalization/Minimization of Substance-Abusing Behavior and/or Relapse Risk

Exercises I.1, I.2, I.3, I.4, I.5, II.3, II.4, II.5, III.5, IV.1, VI.2, VI.3, VI.5, VI.6, VII.3, VII.6, VIII.1, VIII.2, VIII.3, VIII.4, VIII.5, VIII.6, VIII.7, VIII.8, VIII.9, VIII.10, VIII.11

Depression

Exercises I.3, I.4, II.2, III.2, III.3, III.4, III.5, IV.1, IV.2, IV.3, IV.5, IV.6, IV.7, V.1, V.2, V.3, VI.1, VI.2, VII.2, VII.4, VII.5, VII.6, VIII.1, VIII.2, VIII.3, VIII.4, VIII.5, VIII.6, VIII.7, VIII.8, VIII.9, VIII.10, VIII.11

Emotional Isolation

Exercises I.3, I.4, III.1, III.2, III.3, III.4, III.5, IV.1, IV.2, IV.3, IV.4, IV.5, IV.6, VI.2, VI.3, VI.6, VII.1, VII.2, VII.3, VII.5, VII.6, VIII.1, VIII.2, VIII.3, VIII.4, VIII.5, VIII.6, VIII.7, VIII.8, VIII.9, VIII.10, VIII.11, VIII.12

Family Conflict

Exercises I.2, I.4, II.3, II.5, III.5, IV.3, IV.8, IV.9, VI.1, VII.5, VII.6, VIII.3, VIII.5, VIII.6, VIII.7, VIII.8, VIII.9, VIII.10, VIII.12

General Interpersonal Relational Problems

Exercises I.2, I.3, I.4, II.1, II.5, III.3, III.5, IV.3, IV.4, IV.8, VI.3, VI.6, VI.7, VII.2, VII.3, VII.5, VIII.1, VIII.3, VIII.5, VIII.6, VIII.7, VIII.8, VIII.9, VIII.10, VIII.11

Generalized Treatment Resistance

Exercises I.1, I.2, I.3, II.4, II.5, III.5, IV.1, IV.6, V.1, V.2, V.4, VI.3, VI.6, VI.7, VII.3, VII.4, VII.5, VII.6, VIII.1, VIII.2, VIII.3, VIII.4, VIII.5, VIII.6, VIII.7, VIII.8, VIII.9, VIII.10, VIII.11, VIII.12

Grandiosity

Exercises II.4, II.5, III.3, VI.6, VII.5, VII.6, VIII.1, VIII.2, VIII.3, VIII.4, VIII.5, VIII.6, VIII.7, VIII.8, VIII.9, VIII.10, VIII.11

History of Self-Medication for Mood/Pain Problems

Exercises I.1, I.2, III.5, IV.1, IV.3, IV.5, IV.6, V.3, VI.4, VII.1, VII.2, VII.4

Hopelessness

Exercises I.3, II.2, III.1, III.2, III.3, III.4, III.5, IV.2, IV.7, V.1, V.2, V.3, V.4, VI.2, VI.4, VII.1, VII.2, VII.4, VII.5, VIII.1, VIII.2, VIII.3, VIII.4, VIII.5, VIII.6, VIII.7, VIII.9, VIII.10

Impulsivity

Exercises II.4, II.5, IV.1, IV.6, VI.1, VI.2, VI.3, VI.4, VI.5, VI.6, VII.1, VII.2, VII.3, VII.5, VIII.1, VIII.2, VIII.3, VIII.4, VIII.5, VIII.6, VIII.7, VIII.8, VIII.9, VIII.10

Inadequate Support Network

Exercises I.3, I.4, I.5, III.1, III.2, III.3, III.4, IV.2, IV.3, IV.5, IV.6, VI.1, VI.2, VI.3, VI.4, VI.5, VII.3, VII.4, VII.5, VIII.1, VIII.2, VIII.3, VIII.4, VIII.5, VIII.6, VIII.7, VIII.8, VIII.9, VIII.11, VIII.12

Issues of Identity

Exercises I.1, I.4, II.1, II.2, II.3, II.4, III.5, IV.8, V.1, V.2, VII.3, VIII.1, VIII.2, VIII.3, VIII.4, VIII.5, VIII.6, VIII.7, VIII.8, VIII.9, VIII.10, VIII.12

Legal Problems

Exercises I.3, II.4, II.5, III.1, III.4, III.5, IV.3, IV.6, V.1, VI.3, VIII.8

Learned Helplessness

Exercises I.1, I.2, I.3, I.4, II.1, II.2, II.4, III.1, III.2, III.3, III.4, III.5, IV.1, IV.2, IV.6, IV.7, V.1, V.2, V.4, VI.4, VI.6, VII.1, VII.5, VIII.1, VIII.2, VIII.3, VIII.4, VIII.5, VIII.6, VIII.7, VIII.9

Living Environment Deficiencies (Relapse Triggers, Lack of Emotional Support, etc.)

Exercises I.1, I.2, I.3, I.4, I.5, III.1, III.2, III.3, III.4, III.5, IV.1, IV.2, IV.6, V.4, VI.1, VI.2, VI.3, VI.4, VI.5, VII.1, VII.3, VII.4, VII.5, VII.6, VIII.11, VIII.12

Low Self-Esteem

Exercises I.1, I.2, I.3, I.4, II.1, II.2, III.1, III.2, III.3, III.4, III.5, IV.1, IV.2, IV.3, IV.6, IV.7, IV.8, IV.9, V.1, V.2, V.4, VI.2, VI.4, VI.6, VII.1, VII.2, VII.4, VII.5, VII.6, VIII.1, VIII.2, VIII.3, VIII.4, VIII.6, VIII.7, VIII.8, VIII.9, VIII.10, VIII.11, VIII.12

Mania/Hypomania

Exercises II.4, II.5, V.3, VII.1

Medical Issues

Exercises II.4, II.5, III.1, III.4, III.5, IV.1, IV.3, IV.5, IV.6, V.3, VI.3, VI.5, VII.5, VII.3, VII.4

Memory Problems

Exercises V.3, VII.3

Mood Swings

Exercises I.3, III.1, III.4, III.5, IV.7, V.3, VI.2, VII.1, VII.2

Narcissistic Traits

Exercises II.3, II.4, II.5, IV.8, VI.6, VI.7, VII.5, VIII.2, VIII.3, VIII.4, VIII.5, VIII.6, VIII.7, VIII.8, VIII.9, VIII.10, VIII.11

Occupational Problems

Exercises II.1, II.2, II.4, II.5, III.1, III.3, III.4, III.5, IV.1, IV.3, IV.6, IV.8, VI.3, VI.6, VII.3, VII.5, VIII.3, VIII.6, VIII.8, VIII.9, VIII.10, VIII.12

Parent-Child Relational Problems

Exercises I.4, II.1, II.3, II.4, III.1, III.3, III.4, III.5, IV.1, IV.2, IV.4, IV.6, IV.8, VI.3, VI.6, VII.3, VII.5, VII.6, VIII.3, VIII.6, VIII.8, VIII.9, VIII.10, VIII.12

Partner Relational Problems

Exercises I.4, II.1, II.4, II.5, III.1, III.3, III.4, III.5, IV.1, IV.2, IV.4, IV.6, IV.8, VI.3, VI.6, VII.3, VII.5, VII.6, VIII.3, VIII.6, VIII.8, VIII.9, VIII.10, VIII.12

Peer Group Negativity

Exercises I.1, I.2, I.3, I.5, II.5, III.1, III.3, III.5, IV.1, IV.2, IV.6, IV.8, V.1, V.2, V.4, VI.1, VI.3, VI.5, VI.6, VI.7, VIII.1, VIII.2, VIII.3, VIII.4, VIII.5, VIII.6, VIII.7, VIII.8, VIII.9, VIII.10, VIII.11, VIII.12

Poor Social Skills

Exercises I.4, III.1, III.2, III.3, III.4, III.5, IV.1, IV.2, IV.4, IV.6, IV.8, IV.9, VI.5, VI.6, VI.7, VII.2, VII.3, VII.5, VIII.1, VIII.3, VIII.4, VIII.5, VIII.6, VIII.7, VIII.8, VIII.9, VIII.10, VIII.11, VIII.12

Post-acute Withdrawal

Exercises I.1, I.2, I.3, III.1, III.2, III.3, III.4, IV.2, IV.3, IV.5, IV.6, IV.7, V.1, V.2, V.3, VI.1, VI.2, VI.3, VI.4, VI.5, VII.1, VII.2, VII.3, VIII.1, VIII.3, VIII.4, VIII.5, VIII.6, VIII.7, VIII.8, VIII.9, VIII.10, VIII.11

Posttraumatic Stress Issues

Exercises I.4, III.1, III.2, III.3, III.4, III.5, IV.3, IV.7, VI.1, VI.4, VII.2

Recent Bereavement/Loss

Exercises III.2, III.3, III.4, III.5, IV.1, IV.3, VI.1, VI.4, VII.1

Resistance Based on Distorted Beliefs about Substance Abuse/Dependence

Exercises I.1, I.2, I.3, II.4, III.5, IV.1, IV.6, VII.3, VII.4, VII.5, VIII.1, VIII.3, VIII.4, VIII.7, VIII.8, VIII.9, VIII.10, VIII.11, VIII.12

Resistance Based on Distorted Beliefs about Support Groups

Exercises III.4, III.5, IV.2, VIII.1, VIII.2, VIII.3, VIII.4, VIII.5, VIII.6, VIII.7, VIII.8, VIII.9, VIII.10, VIII.11, VIII.12

Shame Issues

Exercises I.1, I.2, I.3, I.4, II.1, III.1, III.2, III.3, III.4, III.5, IV.1, IV.2, IV.7, IV.9, V.1, V.2, VII.1, VII.2, VII.5, VII.6, VIII.1, VIII.2, VIII.3, VIII.4, VIII.5, VIII.6, VIII.7, VIII.8, VIII.9, VIII.10, VIII.11, VIII.12

Sleep Disturbance

Exercises I.3, IV.1, IV.3, IV.5, V.3, VII.1, VII.2, VII.3

Spiritual Confusion

Exercises I.5, II.1, II.2, II.3, II.4, II.5, III.2, III.3, III.4, III.5, IV.1, IV.2, V.1, V.2, VI.5, VII.1, VII.2, VII.5, VIII.1, VIII.2, VIII.3, VIII.4, VIII.5, VIII.6, VIII.7, VIII.8, VIII.9, VIII.10, VIII.11

Substance Abuse

Exercises I.1, I.2, I.3, I.4, I.5, II.3, II.4, II.5, III.1, III.2, III.3, III.4, III.5, IV.1, IV.2, IV.3, IV.5, IV.6, IV.7, IV.8, VI.1, VI.3, VI.6, VI.7, VII.1, VII.2, VII.3, VII.4, VIII.1, VIII.2, VIII.3, VIII.4, VIII.5, VIII.6, VIII.7, VIII.8, VIII.9, VIII.10, VIII.11, VIII.12

Substance Dependence

Exercises I.1, I.2, I.3, I.4, I.5, II.3, II.4, II.5, III.1, III.2, III.3, III.4, III.5, IV.1, IV.2, IV.3, IV.5, IV.6, IV.7, IV.8, VI.1, VI.3, VI.6, VI.7, VII.1, VII.2, VII.3, VII.4, VIII.1, VIII.2, VIII.3, VIII.4, VIII.5, VIII.6, VIII.7, VIII.8, VIII.9, VIII.10, VIII.11, VIII.12

Substance Withdrawal

Exercises I.1, I.2, I.3, IV.1, IV.2, IV.3, IV.5, IV.7, VI.2, VII.4, VIII.1, VIII.2, VIII.3, VIII.4, VIII.5, VIII.6, VIII.7, VIII.8, VIII.9, VIII.10, VIII.11

Suicidality

Exercises III.2, III.4, III.5, IV.1, IV.2, IV.3, IV.7, V.1, V.2, VI.4, VII.1, VII.2, VII.3

Tendency to Repeated Relapse

Exercises I.1, I.2, I.3, I.5, II.3, II.4, II.5, III.1, III.2, III.3, III.4, III.5, IV.1, IV.2, IV.3, IV.5, IV.6, IV.7, IV.9, V.1, V.2, V.3, V.4, VI.1, VI.2, VI.3, VI.4, VI.5, VI.6, VII.1, VII.2, VII.3, VII.5, VIII.1, VIII.2, VIII.3, VIII.4, VIII.5, VIII.6, VIII.7, VIII.8, VIII.9, VIII.10, VIII.11, VIII.12

Treatment/Aftercare Noncompliance

Exercises I.1, I.2, I.3, I.5, II.3, II.4, II.5, III.4, III.5, IV.1, IV.6, V.1, V.4, VI.2, VI.3, VI.5, VII.3, VII.4, VII.5, VIII.1, VIII.2, VIII.3, VIII.4, VIII.6, VIII.7, VIII.8, VIII.9, VIII.10, VIII.11, VIII.12

Unresolved Childhood Trauma

Exercises I.4, II.2, II.3, III.4, III.5, IV.2, IV.8, IV.9, VI.4, VII.1, VII.2, VII.6

Unresolved Grief and Loss

Exercises I.4, III.4, III.5, IV.1, IV.2, IV.9, VI.4, VII.1, VII.2, VII.6, VIII.3

Value Conflicts

Exercises I.5, II.1, II.2, II.3, II.4, II.5, III.4, III.5, IV.1, IV.7, VII.4, VII.5, VII.6, VIII.1, VIII.2, VIII.3, VIII.4, VIII.5, VIII.6, VIII.7, VIII.8, VIII.9, VIII.10, VIII.12

Practice Planners™ offer mental health professionals a full array of practice management tools. These easy-to-use resources include *Treatment Planners*, which cover all the necessary elements for developing formal treatment plans, including detailed problem definitions, long-term goals, short-term objectives, therapeutic interventions, and DSM-IV diagnoses; *Homework Planners* featuring behaviorally-based, ready-to-use assignments which are designed for use between sessions; and *Documentation Sourcebooks* that provide all the forms and records that therapists need to run their practice.

Practice Planners™

For more information on the titles listed below, fill out and return this form to: John Wiley & Sons, Attn: M.Fellin, 605 Third Avenue, New York, NY 10158.

Name _____

Address _____

Address _____

City/State/Zip _____

Telephone _____ Email _____

Please send me more information on:

☐ The Child and Adolescent Psychotherapy Treatment Planner / 240pp / 0-471-15647-7 / $39.95

☐ The Chemical Dependence Treatment Planner / 208pp / 0-471-23795-7 / $39.95

☐ The Continuum of Care Treatment Planner / 208pp / 0-471-19568-5 / $39.95

☐ The Couples Therapy Treatment Planner / 208pp / 0-471-24711-1 / $39.95

☐ The Employee Assistance (EAP) Treatment Planner / 176pp / 0-471-24709-X / $39.95

☐ The Pastoral Counseling Treatment Planner / 208pp / 0-471-25416-9 / $39.95

☐ The Older Adult Psychotherapy Treatment Planner / 176pp / 0-471-29574-4 / $39.95

☐ The Behavioral Medicine Treatment Planner / 176pp / 0-471-31923-6 / $39.95

☐ The Complete Adult Psychotherapy Treatment Planner, Second Edition / 224pp / 0-471-31922-4 / $39.95

☐ TheraScribe® 3.0 for Windows®: The Computerized Assistant to Psychotherapy Treatment Planning Software / 0-471-18415-2 / $450.00 (For network pricing, call 1-800-0655x4708)

☐ TheraBiller™ w/TheraScheduler: The Computerized Mental Health Office Manager Software / 0-471-17102-2 / $599.00 (For network pricing, call 1-800-0655x4708)

☐ The Brief Therapy Homework Planner / 256pp / 0-471-24611-5 / $49.95

☐ The Brief Couples Therapy Homework Planner / 224pp / 0-471-29511-6 / $49.95

☐ The Adolescent Homework Planner / 256pp / 0-471-34465-6 / $49.95

☐ The Child Homework Planner / 256pp / 0-471-32366-7 / $49.95

☐ The Couples & Family Clinical Documentation Sourcebook / 208pp / 0-471-25234-4 / $49.95

☐ The Psychotherapy Documentation Primer / 224pp / 0-471-28990-6 / $39.95

☐ The Clinical Documentation Sourcebook / 256pp / 0-471-17934-5 / $49.95

☐ The The Forensic Documentation Sourcebook / 224pp / 0-471-25459-2 / $75.00

☐ The Chemical Dependence Treatment Documentation Sourcebook / 304pp / 0-471-31285-1 / $49.95

☐ The Child Clinical Documentation Sourcebook / 256pp / 0-471-29111-0 / $49.95

Order the above products through your local bookseller, or by calling 1-800-225-5945, from 8:30 a.m. to 5:30 p.m., est. You can also order via our web site: www.wiley.com/practiceplanners

WILEY
Publishers Since 1807

About the Disk

INTRODUCTION

The forms on the enclosed disk are saved in Microsoft Word for Windows version 7.0. In order to use the forms, you will need to have word processing software capable of reading Microsoft Word for Windows version 7.0 files.

SYSTEM REQUIREMENTS

- IBM PC or compatible computer
- 3.5″ floppy disk drive
- Windows 95 or later
- Microsoft Word for Windows version 7.0 or later or other word processing software capable of reading Microsoft Word for Windows 7.0 files

NOTE: Many popular word processing programs are capable of reading Microsoft Word for Windows 7.0 files. However, users should be aware that a slight amount of formatting might be lost when using a program other than Microsoft Word. If your word processor cannot read Microsoft Word 7.0 files, unformatted text files have been provided in the TXT directory on the floppy disk.

HOW TO INSTALL THE FILES ONTO YOUR COMPUTER

To install the files, follow these instructions:

1. Insert the enclosed disk into the floppy disk drive of your computer.
2. From the Start Menu, choose **Run.**
3. Type **A:\SETUP** and press **OK.**

4. The opening screen of the installation program will appear. Press **OK** to continue.
5. The default destination directory is C:\CHEMICAL. If you wish to change the default destination, you may do so now.
6. Press **OK** to continue. The installation program will copy all files to your hard drive in the C:\CHEMICAL or user-designated directory.

USING THE FILES

Loading Files

To use the word processing files, launch your word processing program. Select **File, Open** from the pull-down menu. Select the appropriate drive and directory. If you installed the files to the default directory, the files will be located in the C:\CHEMICAL directory. A list of files should appear. If you do not see a list of files in the directory, you need to select **WORD DOCUMENT (*.DOC)** under **Files of Type.** Double click on the file you want to open. Edit the file according to your needs.

Printing Files

If you want to print the files, select **File, Print** from the pull-down menu.

Saving Files

When you have finished editing a file, you should save it under a new file name by selecting **File, Save As** from the pull-down menu.

User Assistance

If you need assistance with installation or if you have a damaged disk, please contact Wiley Technical Support at:

Phone:	(212) 850-6753
Fax:	(212) 850-6800 (Attention: Wiley Technical Support)
E-mail:	techhelp@wiley.com

To place additional orders or to request information about other Wiley products, please call (800) 225-5945.

For information about the disk see the **About the Disk** section on pages **301–302.**